FOUR-LEGGED LEGENDS
of COLORADO

BY GAYLE C. SHIRLEY
ILLUSTRATED BY JOHN POTTER

FALCON™
Helena, Montana

*For my grandparents,
Gerald and Evelyn Corbett,
who are legendary people in my eyes*

Copyright © 1994 by Falcon Press Publishing Co., Inc.
Helena and Billings, Montana
Illustrations copyright © 1994 by John Potter

All rights reserved, including the right to reproduce
this book or parts thereof in any form, except for
inclusion of brief quotations in a review.

Shirley, Gayle Corbett.
    Four-legged legends of Colorado / by Gayle C. Shirley.
       p.   cm.
    Includes bibliographical references (p.   ) and index.
    ISBN 1-56044-262-X
    1. Famous animals—Colorado.   I. Title.
QL793.S47   1994
818'.540308036—dc20   94-30023
                                                                              CIP

Printed in the United States of America

Falcon Press Publishing Co., Inc.
P.O. Box 1718
Helena, Montana 59624
1-800-582-2665

Contents

Acknowledgments iv

Introduction vi

Tall Bull: Battle Trophy 1

Old Mose: Man Killer 11

Buff and Blaze: Fatal Foes 21

Prunes: Prospector's Partner 27

Bum and Shorty: Inseparable Pals 37

Skipper: War Veteran 43

Hambone: Jumpin' Fool 53

Shep: Turnpike Mascot 61

Elijah: Harried Hermit 67

Snippy: Headless Hoax? 77

Ralphie: Buffaloes' Gal 91

Bo: Whitewater Hero 99

Yogi: Super Sleuth 103

Bibliography 110

Index 117

ACKNOWLEDGMENTS

I had the help of many generous people while writing *Four-Legged Legends of Colorado*. For sharing their knowledge, helping to locate research materials, and reviewing parts of the manuscript for accuracy, I'd like to thank Kathy Mora, Great Falls (Montana) Public Library; the staff of the Colorado Historical Society, Denver, including Rebecca Lintz and Margaret Walsh; Beth Armstrong, Boulder (Colorado) Public Library; Carol Davis, South Park Historical Foundation Inc., Fairplay, Colorado; Paul Fees, Curator, Buffalo Bill Museum, Cody, Wyoming; Toni Gatzen, Colorado Department of Transportation, Denver; Eleanor Gehres, Western History Department, Denver Public Library; Herbert Mullican, Jr., Frederick, Maryland; Officer Jerry Nichols, Aurora (Colorado) Police Department, K-9 Unit; Hazel Petty, San Luis Valley History Center, Alamosa, Colorado; Dave Plati, University of Colorado Athletics Department, Boulder; Charlotte Smokler, Boulder *Daily Camera*; Joanna Stout, Fairplay; Elise Tiedt, Pikes Peak Library District, Local History Division, Colorado Springs, Colorado; Jessie Vicha, McDowell & Piasecki Food Communications, Chicago; and Dennis Webb, *Glenwood Post*, Glenwood Springs, Colorado.

Gayle C. Shirley
June 1994

"What is man without the beasts?
If all the beasts were gone,
man would die from a great loneliness of spirit.
For whatever happens to the beasts
happens to man."

Chief Seattle
1854

INTRODUCTION

Ever since man uttered his first words, he's considered himself supreme ruler of the natural world. But he's first and foremost an animal. He can't avoid sharing important, if ambivalent, relationships with the rest of the species that inhabit the earth.

Generally, man tends to perceive the rest of the animal kingdom in one of four ways: as pets, prey, pests, or slaves. And sometimes the boundaries between these grow murky. Twelve thousand years ago, man befriended the dog, his faithful companion and "best friend." Yet the wolf, the dog's close cousin, has long inspired more hatred than almost any other creature. He's even the villain of many of our traditional fairy tales.

We humans can't help but be fascinated by animals. We search for and celebrate their likenesses to us but grow uneasy with their differences. Author Edith Wharton once wrote in her diary:

> I am secretly afraid of animals—of all animals except dogs, and even of some dogs. I think it is because of the us-ness in their eyes, with the underlying not-us-ness which belies it, and is so tragic a reminder of the lost age when we human beings branched off and left them: left them to eternal inarticulateness and slavery. "Why?" their eyes seem to ask us.

In *Four-Legged Legends of Colorado*, you'll get a sense of this love-hate relationship man has with his fellow beings. Some of the animals featured here were cherished for their loyalty or admired for their strength or intelligence. Others were reviled because their efforts to survive interfered with our own interests.

As you read this book, you'll realize that man's attitudes toward animals can change over time. Where once we did our best to exterminate the wolves and grizzlies, today we afford them special protection, to make sure they stay with us in this world. But that's not to say those deep, dark feelings don't still exist. We continue to weigh our responsibility to the creatures we walk among. Is it our job to prevent them from extinction? Even if the needs of those species conflict with our own? By now we know there are no easy answers.

The animals whose stories you're about to read were selected because they stood out, even among their own kind, and captured our imaginations. All of them achieved some measure of fame not only in Colorado, but nationwide. Because we thought them unique, we bestowed names upon them and kept their legends alive. Even with the passage of decades, they still stir our hearts.

TALL BULL

BATTLE TROPHY

"God forbid that I should go to any heaven in which there are no horses."

Robert Graham
in a letter to Theodore Roosevelt

William F. Cody crouched amid the litter of the hastily abandoned Indian camp and studied the odd footprint. This was no moccasin track. It was the imprint of a woman's shoe—and its meaning was unmistakable. Tall Bull and his band of Cheyennes had taken a white settler captive. The mission of the Fifth Cavalry, to pursue and subdue the band, grew suddenly more urgent. Someone had to rescue that poor, frightened woman.

The soldiers of the Fifth, under the command of Major General Eugene Carr, had left Fort McPherson, Nebraska, a month earlier—on June 9, 1869—after learning that the Cheyennes were camped at the headwaters of the Republican River. Cody, 23, accompanied the expedition as Carr's chief scout. He also was expected to keep the troops supplied with buffalo meat, giving him plenty of opportunities to show off the skills that had earned him the nickname "Buffalo Bill."

When the Indians learned of the cavalry's approach, they retreated northward, and Carr and his men followed as quickly as possible, hoping to intercept them before they crossed the South Platte River. The thirsty troopers covered 150 miles in four days under a blistering sun. Finally, on July 11, a Pawnee scout reported Tall Bull's camp only a few miles ahead. It was nestled among the sand hills of northeastern Colorado at a watering place known as Summit Springs.

Cody recommended that the cavalry detour around the Cheyennes—stealthily slipping behind ridges and through ravines—so that it could block their retreat to the river and take them by surprise.

"Acting on my suggestion, [Carr] made a circuit to the north, believing that if the Indians had their scouts out, they would naturally be watching in the direction whence they had come," Cody later recalled.

The cavalrymen halted on the summit of a hill overlooking Tall Bull's unsuspecting camp. It was a pleasant summer day. The Cheyennes and some of their Sioux allies lounged in the shade of their lodges, chatting and smoking. Many of their ponies were tied nearby, dozing in the sun. Others grazed in large herds on a hillside about two miles away.

At about two o'clock in the afternoon, Carr commanded the bugler to sound the charge. In broad daylight, almost three hundred horsemen galloped undetected across the open plain that lay between them and the doomed village. A furious wind drowned out their shouts and the pounding of their horses' hooves.

Lieutenant George Price, the regimental historian, later described the scene with pride.

> The chief trumpeter was ordered to sound the charge. Only those who were near him could hear the short sharp notes, but every man saw him going through the motions. That was enough. All knew that there was only one call to sound then; and away dashed the gallant troopers in one of the most superb charges ever made by the Fifth Cavalry.

Just as planned, the attack was a complete surprise. One Cheyenne, Two Crows, was sitting in his lodge talking when he heard someone shout, "People are coming!" He thought nothing of it and continued his conversation. When he heard gunshots, he rushed outside. Soldiers were pouring into the village. Panicked warriors were scrambling for their weapons and horses. Women and children were screaming, and many were running away on foot to hide in the bluffs.

The fight was short and bloody. When it ended, fifty-two Indians lay dead, and seventeen women and children were prisoners. The Fifth Cavalry, however, emerged almost unscathed. Not a single soldier had died, and only one man was wounded—slightly scratched by an arrow.

The soldiers discovered *two* white captives in the camp. One of them, a Mrs. Suzannah Alderdice, had been killed early in the battle by an Indian woman—some said it was Tall Bull's wife—who had bashed her in the head with a tomahawk. The other woman, a Mrs. G. Weichel, had barely escaped a similar fate. She was taken to Fort Sedgwick, Colorado, to recover from her wounds, and she later married the hospital steward who took care of her there.

In the middle of this chaos, Cody played a part in another deadly drama. No one knows exactly what happened. Various accounts of the battle tell the story differently. But Major Carr, in his official report, put it this way:

> "Tall Bull" the chief, finding how matters were going, determined to die. He had a little daughter on his horse and one of his wives on another. He gave the daughter to his wife and told her to escape and take the white woman who was prisoner, and she might use her to make terms for herself when peace was made. The wife begged him to escape with her, but he shut his ears, killed his horse, and she saw him killed fighting. She then surrendered and was saved with her daughter of eight and brother of twelve years.

More than one person tried to take the credit for killing the notorious Tall Bull, but Carr later said there was "no doubt that Buffalo Bill killed the chief." Yet, as Cody first told the story, he was more interested in Tall Bull's horse than he was in the Cheyenne warrior.

> I was in the skirmish line, and I noticed an Indian, who was riding a large bay horse, and giving orders to his men in his own language—which I could occasionally understand—telling them that they had lost everything, that they were ruined, and he entreated them to follow him, and fight until

they died. His horse was an extraordinary one, fleet as the wind, dashing here and there, and I determined to capture him if possible, but I was afraid to fire at the Indian for fear of killing his horse.

I noticed that the Indian, as he rode around the skirmish line, passed the head of a ravine not far distant, and it occurred to me that if I could dismount and creep into the ravine I could, as he passed there, easily drop him from his saddle without danger of hitting his horse. Accordingly, I crept into and secreted myself in the ravine... and I waited there until Mr. Chief came riding by.

When he was not more than thirty yards distant I fired, and the next moment he tumbled from his saddle, and the horse kept on without his rider.... He galloped toward our men, by one of whom he was caught.... The Sergeant knew that I had been trying to get the animal and having seen me kill his rider, he handed him over to me at once....

I jumped on his back and rode him down to the spot where the prisoners were corralled. One of the squaws... suddenly began crying in a pitiful and hysterical manner at the sight of this horse, and upon inquiry I found that she was Tall Bull's wife.... She stated that this was her husband's favorite war horse, and that only a short time ago she had seen Tall Bull riding him. I gave her to understand that her liege lord had passed in his mortal chips... and I informed her that henceforth I should call the gallant steed "Tall Bull" in honor of her husband.

Did Chief Tall Bull kill his horse as Carr reported or not? Did he change horses sometime during the battle? Did the horse captured by Cody belong to some other warrior? No one will ever know the answers to these questions now. What is known for a fact is that Cody emerged from the Battle of Summit Springs with a horse that would eventually gain a reputation as the fastest steed west of the Mississippi. Cody liked to ride it bareback at full speed, holding on to its mane and jumping to the ground and up again in a stunt he would later perform with other horses in his Wild West Show. He won many a bet from those foolish enough to challenge him and Tall Bull to a race.

In the fall of 1870, after an expensive night of revelry, Cody sold Tall Bull to a cavalryman "to raise necessary funds." One account said those funds were used to buy some furniture he'd promised to bring home to his wife. It seems odd that Cody would so easily relinquish a horse he took such pains to acquire.

Buffalo Bill spent most of his life on horseback—as a Pony Express rider, buffalo hunter for the Kansas Pacific Railroad, guide and scout for the U.S. Cavalry, and finally performer in his own popular Wild West Show. He was a superb horseman, and several of his mounts—including Tall Bull—loped their way into the pages of history.

Cody acquired the nickname "Buffalo Bill" while riding Brigham, a horse he got from a Ute Indian and named for the Mormon leader, Brigham Young. It was aboard this celebrated steed that he killed 4,280 buffalo in eight months to feed workers laying the tracks of the Kansas Pacific Railroad. Cody once said Brigham was "the best horse I ever owned or saw for buffalo chasing."

When the Kansas Pacific suspended work in 1868, Cody reluctantly raffled off Brigham to get the money he needed to take his wife and baby to Leavenworth for the winter. The very next year, shortly before the Battle of Summit Springs, he traded a Pawnee for a horse he named Buckskin Joe. This "rather sorry looking" animal soon gained a reputation as the greatest long-distance horse of its day, a tremendous asset on a frontier fraught with danger. When the horse died, a tombstone erected over its grave read:

> Old Buckskin Joe, the horse that on several occasions saved the life of Buffalo Bill by carrying him safely out of range of Indian bullets. Died of old age, 1882.

Cody owned many other horses: Powder Face, also acquired during the Battle of Summit Springs, figured prominently in the dime novels that Ned Buntline wrote about Buffalo Bill. Tucker, a handsome white horse, appeared in a famous portrait of Cody painted in 1889 by artist Rosa Bonheur. Billy, also white, probably performed in more cities and before more aristocrats than any of Cody's other mounts. Duke, a magnificent chestnut, was one of the most beautiful horses Cody ever owned.

And then there was Charlie, a horse Cody claimed had "almost human intelligence," as well as extraordinary speed, endurance, and fidelity. The animal starred in the first Wild West shows and was perhaps the most publicized horse of its day. The pair were pals for at least fourteen years. When Charlie died aboard a ship coming home from Europe, Cody delivered an emotional eulogy.

Old fellow, your journeys are over.... Willing speed, tireless courage... you have never failed me. Ah, Charlie, old fellow, I have had many friends, but few of whom I could say that... I loved you as you loved me. Men tell me you have no soul; but if there is a heaven and scouts can enter there, I'll wait at the gate for you, old friend.

Cody died in Denver on January 10, 1917. A white horse wearing an empty saddle escorted the legendary Buffalo Bill to his grave on Lookout Mountain, just west of town.

Old Mose

Man Killer

"That old bear was a heap more cunning than a fox.... I had a wholesome respect for him, and after looking his carcass over I am free to say that I am thankful that I never came face to face with him."

C.W. Talbot
Colorado prospector

The three deer hunters probably never dreamed that this late November day in 1883 would hold such horror. In fact, it seemed an ideal day for hunting. The sky was a brittle porcelain blue, and there was no breeze to carry their scent and spook their prey. As they hiked through the heavy timber of south-central Colorado, Jake Radliff, Henry Seymour, and John Cory decided to split up and hunt alone. They soon lost sight of each other in the trees.

It wasn't long before Seymour heard a gunshot and a cry for help. He took off in the direction of the sounds, weaving through the underbrush and between the trunks of spruce and aspen. His insides must have twisted in fear when he came upon the mutilated body of Radliff lying in a clearing. The broken and bleeding man was still alive. Later, he would regain consciousness long enough to tell a gruesome story.

Radliff had been headed down a small gully when he noticed a pile of freshly turned dirt. Thinking it might be a prospecting hole, he went to investigate. What he found instead was a bear's den, and as he soon discovered, the bear itself was not far away, gathering twigs and leaves to line its winter bed.

Before Radliff could retreat, the bear charged. The hunter's hometown newspaper, the *Fairplay Flume*, vividly described the attack.

> Mr. Radliff had only time to draw up his gun and fire at random when the bear was so near that he had to push it off with his gun to prevent its ponderous claws tearing him.... He had pushed off the bear several times... when the brute caught his ankle with its paw, and breaking the bones like twigs tossed the hunter into the air six feet. As he fell to the ground the brute pounced upon him, crunching the bones of his legs, tearing his cheek, and clawing his body frightfully. Mr. Radliff was perfectly conscious. He knew his danger, uttered repeated cries and endeavored to rise and escape but the infuriated brute again tossed him in the air, and as he fell bit him nearly from ear to ear and tore off his scalp. Then the poor victim... lost consciousness.

Seymour and Cory improvised a stretcher by tying a blanket between two aspen poles. As tenderly as possible, they carried their companion back to camp and, wrapping him in the blanket, laid him in the back of their horse-drawn wagon. They headed down the mountain as swiftly as they dared and arrived at the IM Ranch on Badger Creek late in the evening. One of the cowboys at the ranch later reported that Radliff was bleeding so heavily that the blanket was soaked and blood was oozing from the wagon box.

The young mistress of the ranch did all she could to bind Radliff's wounds and relieve his pain. Meanwhile, the cowboy rode to the nearest railway station, forty-five miles away, to send a telegram to the Fairplay doctor. The physician reached the depot at one in the morning. On horseback, the two galloped for hours—over ridges and down arroyos—to the ranch. They arrived exhausted and saddle-sore, just as the sun peeked over the horizon.

The doctor gingerly examined Radliff's wounds. The suffering man had a deep bite in the back of his neck. His scalp had almost been ripped off, one arm was cut and broken and torn loose at the shoulder, both thighs had been shredded, and one leg was broken in two places. Conscious but in agony, Radliff recounted his terrible ordeal.

The doctor decided to move his patient to Fairplay, but Radliff died en route. His last words, whispered while he was still at the ranch, were "Boys, don't hunt that bear."

None of the three hunters mentioned what kind of bear killed Radliff, but the animal's tracks measured ten inches in diameter, making it large even for a grizzly. Many area ranchers suspected this was the same bear that had been tearing down their fences and gorging on their cattle since at least 1878—a grizzly known as Old

Mose. Some said the animal was named by two old-timers who were impressed with the way the bear would mosey into a miner's camp, scare the man witless, and then mosey off again, seemingly pleased with its prank. Others say the animal was named after a notorious bear that had once ranged northwestern Colorado.

With the death of Radliff, Old Mose became a marked bear. For the next two decades, hunters roamed from Leadville to Monte Vista and from Gunnison to Canon City in pursuit of the wily fugitive. Others would set increasingly elaborate traps, but, as one newspaper reported,

> ...the old bear seemed to know them and their deadly workings. Some way he knew at once if they were set or sprung, and if sprung, he would walk into them and help himself to the bait. If set, his tracks would show how he had circled the trap and gone his way.

One cattleman near Fairplay constructed a three-foot-high pen with a gap in it. He put a dead cow in the enclosure and a steel trap at its entrance. Old Mose outwitted the man three times. He simply reached over the wall with one huge paw and lifted the carcass out.

The owner of the Stirrup Ranch at the foot of Black Mountain, Wharton Pigg, came the closest to success. He had become obsessed with hunting the big grizzly and had studied its movements and the extent of its territory. With this knowledge, he determined approximately when Old Mose would next visit Black Mountain, and he told one of his hired hands to set a trap. This man, knowing that the bear had often visited a particular lake, placed his trap in the shallow water along its shore.

Every morning, someone from the ranch would climb a hillside to check the trap. One day, a boy named John Douglas was sent to do the honors, and to his delight, he was the one to carry back the good news. He had seen a giant of a bear thrashing about in the water, its paw clamped in steel jaws.

At the ranch house, excited men sprinted for their guns. But when they reached the trap, Old Mose was gone—except, that is, for two toes from his right hind foot which he had chewed off and left in the trap. From then on, the grizzly's tracks were even easier to identify.

By 1904, Old Mose had been credited with killing eight hundred head of livestock valued at $30,000 and at least two men besides Radliff. When a skeleton was discovered lying beside a rusted Winchester rifle on Cameron Mountain, the remains were identified as those of a hunter named James Asher, and his death was attributed to Old Mose. So was that of some unfortunate cowboy whose bones were found, along with boots and spurs, just north of Guffey in 1903. Other hunters who went after the grizzly and never returned were assumed—rightly or wrongly—to be its victims.

Old Mose, a Denver newspaper claimed, was "the most dreaded grizzly bear in the entire United States." In the course of his long and savage career, he was

> ...shot through and through times without number, baited with every device and cunning known to the trapper; chased by demon posses of cowboys and ranchers bent upon his extermination, and in all this he has met them

with superior generalship, cunning unexcelled, knowledge supreme.

All that ended in 1904, when a hunter named James W. Anthony moved to Canon City from Boise, Idaho. He later wrote:

> I brought along a pack of bear dogs. When this became generally known about the first thing a new acquaintance would ask would be "Why don't you kill Old Mose?" I heard this so often I finally declared I thought I must be the only friend Old Mose had.

He didn't remain a friend for long. Anthony soon met rancher Pigg, who invited the newcomer to help stalk the big bear, using the Stirrup Ranch as home base. Beginning in early April, the pair scoured the hills on horseback for signs of their quarry. Finally, on April 27, they found a set of huge grizzly tracks. They returned to the ranch for the dogs.

For the next two days, the hunters followed the tracks across creeks, through fences, down gullies, and along ridges. On the morning of April 30, they skirted Black Mountain. When they stopped for lunch at one o'clock, Anthony pulled dried bear meat from his saddlebags and joked, "Let us eat some of this for medicine," in the Indian sense of the word. Back on the trail, the two men went about a fourth of a mile before the dogs discovered fresh tracks. Anthony described what happened next.

> The dogs were crazily excited by the scent of the bear, jumping, squirming, barking, and

crying to be free, and as fast as one was slipped [out of its collar], would disappear among the trees on the track. I had eight dogs, four couples, and by the time the last collar was off and couplings and rope tied on the saddle, the leaders had a good start of us.... I followed Ray, my best dog, paid no attention to the others, and Mr. Pigg kept with me. As soon as Ray and his following, Ring, Dummit, and Ginger had the tracks straightened and apparently going toward Black Mountain, Mr. Pigg rode rapidly in that direction, along the ridge.... I followed for a few rods, then rode to the left a few rods and stopped and listened. I was on the edge of a little cliff, and below me and a little to the right, perhaps fifteen rods [about eighty-two yards] away, but out of sight in a dense growth of spruce and aspen, were my dogs, barking savagely. I knew they were fighting him close up, that the bear was bayed, and barring mishaps as good as killed.

Anthony dismounted, slipped off his gloves, and loaded a cartridge into the chamber of his rifle. Later, he told the *Denver Times*:

> I... soon came upon [the] four... dogs in a grove of quaking asp, where they surrounded the biggest bear I ever saw in my life. At first he took no notice of me and paid but little attention to the dogs while he walked along, though they were pulling fur every minute. I fired at about seventy yards. Then I let go three more in quick succession, all of which

were hits, but none fatal. He stood on his haunches and looked at me, dropped down and then started toward me. At about three rods [a little more than sixteen yards] I took careful aim with my .30-40 Winchester. At this distance [bears] generally make a rush upon a man. I got him between the eyes and he fell without a quiver.... It took seven of us, and with a heap of labor, to get him to Stirrup ranch.

Pigg, though disappointed that he hadn't had the honor of firing the fatal shot, hauled the huge carcass to Canon City in a wagon and hung it up for display at the Wright & Morgan Market. More than three thousand people came to gawk, according to *The Denver Post*. The outlaw bear weighed 875 pounds minus blood and entrails. Alive, folks guessed, it must have weighed about 1,200 pounds—or about double the size of the average full-grown grizzly. And this after months of hibernation! The *Post* dared to call it "the largest bear ever killed in Colorado."

From nose to tail, the hide measured ten feet, four inches long, and the claws were five inches long. The bear was thought to have been about thirty-five to forty years old. For days, markets throughout the area sold bear meat that was reputed to be that of Old Mose.

Anthony kept Old Mose's hide and skull and in his will bequeathed them to the Museum of Vertebrate Zoology in Berkeley, California. They remain in the museum's collection today and are available to researchers for study. The brain was turned over to Dr. Ellsworth Lancaster, a professor at Colorado College in Colorado Springs and a specialist in psychology and neuroanatomy. He was surprised at how small the brain was. It weighed only fifteen ounces. That meant that the bear's brain-to-body ratio—a sign of intelligence, he claimed—was less than one to a thousand, while the ratio of a man's brain to his body is one to forty-five. He also found that four inches of "porous, or cellular, structure" protected the front end of the brain. That, he said, "explains why [the hunter] finds it so hard to kill the grizzly by firing a ball into the front of the head."

According to Lancaster, Old Mose's brain indicated that the bear had exceptionally good senses of smell and hearing and well-developed motor abilities. The cortex, however, was under-developed, which meant the infamous bear was "cunning but not intelligent."

Based upon his examination, the professor reached this charitable conclusion:

> This bear did not reason, did not love or hate, probably, and was mild and peaceable if left alone. If frightened or injured or hungry, his instincts said run, crush or kill.

And that's exactly what Old Mose did.

BUFF AND BLAZE
FATAL FOES

> *"Although a domestic animal, the longhorn was always courageous enough to stand and face the grizzly singly on any field of battle. This was undoubtedly due to the longhorn being endowed with the spirit of self-preservation, plus the knowledge and fighting blood gained through generation after generation of battle for existence against drought, flood, blizzard, and carnivorous enemies."*
>
> W.P. Hubbard
> *Notorious Grizzly Bears*

Lon Duncan hid behind a pile of boulders within sight of the mineral spring and waited to ambush his prey—an outlaw grizzly known as Buff. Named for its light yellowish-brown coat, the bear had destroyed close to two hundred cattle, sheep, and horses in the

San Juan country of southwestern Colorado. Stockmen had offered a $750 reward for its death.

As this day in 1894 dawned, Duncan could just make out Buff's tracks leading to and from the spring. Obviously, the animal had come to drink during the night. But Duncan knew the bear usually visited the spot a couple of times before moving on to other parts of its territory, so he decided to sit tight. He didn't realize he was about to witness a bloody duel to the death.

After a while, the hunter heard something coming. He tensed and raised his rifle to his shoulder, but the animal that stepped into the clearing around the spring was no grizzly. It was a big, blaze-faced, roan-colored bull with white hindquarters and legs. Duncan recognized it as a Hereford-Longhorn cross that area cattlemen called Blaze. It had a reputation for being wild, tough, and cagey, with battle scars criss-crossing its body to prove it. It had dodged every roundup for twelve years.

Just as the bull was about to drink, it whirled with a snort and threw up its head. The hair on its neck stood straight up, and its nostrils flared. It looked as defiant as any bull that ever faced a matador in the ring.

Duncan followed the bull's gaze and was surprised to see Buff standing on his hind legs at the entrance to the little gully in which the spring lay. The bear stared at the bull intently. He seemed to realize that he had the advantage, that he blocked the only way to escape.

Blaze snorted, pawed the ground, and swung his sharp horns from side to side. Despite the warning, Buff dropped to all fours and cautiously approached. When the bear got to within a few feet, Blaze charged. Buff sent him tumbling to the ground with one swipe of his claws.

As he fell, Blaze lashed out with his back hooves, leaving deep slashes on the grizzly's chest. The bear went over backwards with a bawl of pain and rage. Blaze got to his feet first. When the bear turned to face him, he lunged forward and drove one horn deep into Buff's shoulder. With a powerful flip of his head, he tore himself free just as the bear sunk its teeth into him. The two animals separated and began circling each other warily.

W.P. Hubbard described the next round of battle in his book *Notorious Grizzly Bears*.

> After several threatening starts on the part of each of them, the bull followed through. Buff half rose as he turned sideways to avoid the charge, but one horn caught him just under the left front leg, going clear through the leg muscle and coming out along the shoulder. Buff bawled with rage, hooked his claws into Blaze's side and back, and tried to bite the top of the bull's neck just back of the head. If he had succeeded, he would have probably broken the bull's neck. The constant moving of Blaze, along with the horn against [Buff's] shoulder, prevented this. Consequently, he vented his fury by clawing and biting Blaze's shoulder and side as best he could. They were stuck in that position for a good quarter-minute.... Finally Blaze gave a mighty uplift with his head and moved sideways, drawing the horn free. Then he struck savagely at Buff with a sharp hoof, missed, and backed away.
>
> Both of them were covered in blood. The left side of Blaze's neck and shoulder was a

mass of torn flesh where the bear had raked and pounded him with claws and paws. Blood ran from gashes and horn punctures on Buff's chest, sides, and shoulders.

The two foes didn't stay apart long. In the ensuing combat, Blaze threw the grizzly against a fallen tree, impaling him on one of its branches. The limb went in behind Buff's ribs and came out behind his left shoulder. The force of the fall broke it from the tree so that both ends protruded from Buff's body.

After lying beside the log for several moments, Buff climbed to his feet and wobbled toward Blaze. Again, the bull gored him with one horn and then pivoted free. As they parted, the grizzly tore the bull's throat open, and Blaze responded by ripping a gash in Buff's belly with his hooves. Parts of the bear's entrails dragged on the ground. The end of the battle was near. Hubbard described it like this:

> Suddenly [Buff] dropped to the ground. Once he tried to rise, but his life's blood was about gone. He sank back, his head slumped forward. He was dead.
>
> Blaze was standing spraddle-legged, his head down, and was trembling all over. Finally he stumbled over to the grizzly. Amid a mixture of groaning snorts, he jabbed at him with a horn. Blaze, bleeding badly, was about done for. Hesitantly, he moved [out of the gully] and disappeared from view.
>
> Duncan grabbed his rifle and ran down a draw to the canyon.... He came upon Blaze beside a huge rock. He, too, was dead.

This was one duel to the death with no survivors.

Duncan had the heads of Blaze and Buff mounted just as they were—minus eyes and chunks of flesh. He estimated that the bull had weighed about 1,500 pounds. The horns measured three feet ten inches from tip to tip. Buff weighed 887 pounds and had been between fifteen and eighteen years old. Several claws on his forepaws had recently been broken off, rendering him slightly less dangerous than usual. The tree limb, once it was pulled from the bear's body, measured three feet one inch long, and Duncan hung it over his fireplace for years. It had cracked two of Buff's ribs and torn a vein leading to the heart.

In researching outlaw grizzlies for his book, Hubbard said he found only one—Buff—that had been killed by another animal. He heard the story of the deadly duel straight from Duncan, its only eyewitness.

PRUNES

PROSPECTOR'S PARTNER

"The history of Colorado is punctuated with anecdotes about burros and mules. They, not dogs, were the pioneers' best friends. They shared life, and between beast and man, there was a devotion and understanding that enabled both to survive on the frontier."

Ralph C. Taylor
The Pueblo Chieftain
April 9, 1978

Rupert Sherwood's eightieth birthday party was a jolly affair—the last, in fact, that the old prospector would share with his partner of fifty years. To celebrate, Sherwood and his friends crowded into his little cabin in Fairplay, Colorado, to feast on roast venison and swig bootleg liquor. His partner, a shaggy pack burro named Prunes, spent that nippy November evening in 1929 outside munching on oats instead.

In the midst of the revelry, Sherwood noticed that the burro was having trouble chewing its meal. So the next morning he took a peek at its mouth. The poor old creature, believed to be sixty-two years old itself, had lost every tooth in its head.

"Too bad they can't make false teeth for burros," Sherwood later told *The Denver Post*. "Prunes would be as frisky as a colt right now if his crunchers hadn't failed him."

In the animal kingdom, a creature with no teeth faces a slow death by starvation. Sherwood couldn't bear to think of that happening to Prunes. But he also couldn't bear the wind, snow, and ice of South Park winters anymore, and he had planned to make his customary trip to Denver to spend the season with friends.

In past winters, Prunes had easily survived his master's absences by begging handouts from the kind townspeople of Fairplay and nearby Alma. The burro would make the rounds of the ramshackle mining camps every day, stomping his front hoof on the back steps of cabins to announce his visits. The residents—especially the children—responded with a little hay, biscuits, and especially flapjacks. One woman cooked him a bowl of oatmeal every morning.

"Everybody fed him," Sherwood said. "He'd eat anything. Flapjacks in particular—cold or hot. Fry 'em in a skillet, with sowbelly grease, an' Prunes would heehaw with delight!"

Now, as Sherwood prepared to leave for Denver yet again, he begged his friends to look after his faithful companion. With sad foreboding, he wished his burro the best and said farewell until spring.

But the best was not to be. A fierce blizzard battered central Colorado that winter and buried it under twenty-foot drifts of snow. For a week the wind howled, and the bitter cold drove people indoors to huddle beside their wood stoves. Prunes sought shelter, too. Cold and hungry, he holed up in an old abandoned shed. But the wind slammed the door shut, and Prunes's haven became a prison.

When the storm ended, people began to fret about Prunes. He was, after all, the town pet, and no one had seen him for several days. Folks pulled on galoshes, coats, and gloves and organized a search. Finally, a group of children discovered Prunes in the shed—wretched, gaunt, and weak with hunger. "He was nearly done for," Sherwood later recalled. Everyone showered the pitiful beast with flapjacks, and Prunes managed to survive the winter. But it was obvious he would never be his sociable old self again.

When Sherwood returned to Fairplay in May, Prunes managed a weak heehaw in welcome. The old man must have been grief-stricken at the sight of his feeble friend. Before long, someone called a meeting of the miners, and they decided the humane thing to do was to put Prunes out of his misery.

Sherwood wept.

"We're both oldtimers from away back," he said. "Why, old Prunes has packed for every mine Park County ever had.... Lord! I hate to see 'im killed, but I suppose it's best."

Prunes, long-eared pioneer of the Colorado mines, was shot, and his carcass was taken to the town dump. Leading newspapers in the state carried the news of his death, for Prunes had already become a legend.

Prunes reportedly was born in 1867 near the Buckskin Joe mine about seven miles northwest of Fairplay. His name was inspired by the dark brown color of his shaggy coat, a color reminiscent of dried plums. In 1879, Sherwood bought the jack burro for ten dollars from a pair of miners in Alma who had decided to sell their claims.

Only twenty-nine years old, Sherwood had already lived a difficult and adventurous life. He was born November 24, 1849, on a little farm near Beloit, Wisconsin. His father died when he was five, and his mother followed three or four years later. But Sherwood had no intention of languishing in an orphanage. He "got out and rustled a living," as he described it, and in 1862—at the age of twelve—he crossed the plains to Colorado with a large herd of horses that was on its way to the California market. He worked as a "coper," which meant he was responsible for currying the horses and dressing their wounds so that they would look their best for prospective buyers.

Perhaps in part because of Sherwood's hard work, his employer managed to sell the entire herd during a stopover in Denver. For the next several years, young Sherwood wandered from Colorado to Kansas to Wisconsin, hunting, trapping, and living the "open-hearted, carefree life of a bachelor." Finally, in 1877, the prospect of gold lured him to Colorado to stay.

Sherwood proved to be moderately successful as a prospector and miner in the Leadville, Fairplay, and Alma districts. He earned $15,000 selling his most profitable claim. By the time he and Prunes teamed up, the plucky burro had already hauled ore for the Dolly Varden, Mosquito, Home Sweet Home, and Buckskin mines. Even *The Denver Post* recognized the animal's contributions. It said:

> Prunes worked and associated with early miners as if it were his solemn obligation, equally with theirs, to build trails, pack down the ore and help mold the struggling Colorado territory into the great state it is today.

Now, Prunes and his new partner roamed the mountains together, Sherwood keeping an eye out for the glint of gold, and Prunes carrying everything a prospector might need: blankets, a gold pan, a frying pan, a coffee pot, an ax, a pick, a shovel, rope, flour, bacon, coffee, sugar—and, of course, oats.

"He was good," Sherwood said. "Surefooted as a goat, willing and able, too.... Like any other jack but tougher, fit to stand anything and like it."

In her booklet *Two Burros of Fairplay*, Caroline Bancroft described the teamwork involved in mining.

> It was hard work, washing gold out of the dirt with only a gold pan. Many prospectors built "Long Toms" or sluice boxes close to the streams. "Long Toms" were made out of hollowed-out logs and rocked back and forth with a long, upright handle to slosh the water and gravel out. Sluice boxes were fashioned from strips of lumber which led the water and gravel down a trough set with steps or riffles in it. The gravel and water rushed on, but the gold and iron, being heavier, stuck behind the riffles. Then mercury was used to absorb the gold into a ball. Both "Long Toms" and sluice boxes made it easier to wash the gold from the earth.
>
> If Rupe [Sherwood] found a claim that seemed rich enough to work for some time, he used the sluice box method, and Prunes had the chore of dragging felled trees and lumber into place.

To deal with some smaller claims, Sherwood harnessed Prunes to his pick, and the burro pulled it back and forth like a plow until the ground was loose and his master could haul loads of the dirt to a nearby stream for washing. Prunes also helped drag away stones too big for Sherwood to lift. And sometimes Sherwood would tie a note to Prunes's halter and send him into town for provisions. The burro would wait patiently in front of the general store until the storekeeper filled Sherwood's order and loaded everything onto Prunes's back. Then the reliable animal would pick his way back up the trail—all for a pat on the head and a few lumps of sugar.

By the time World War I broke out, the demand for gold and silver had dropped considerably, and a man couldn't get a decent price for the ore he had to work so hard to unearth. Sherwood and his only companion were getting old now. They gave up prospecting and lazed away the summer days, enjoying the beauty of the Colorado mountains.

Prunes's death was hard on Sherwood, and everyone agreed that the town dump wasn't a fitting resting place for this faithful and hard-working creature. So the people of Alma and Fairplay started collecting money to build a monument to their old friend. The concrete memorial was erected beside one of the main streets of Fairplay, where it stands to this day. It reads:

PRUNES
A BURRO
1867-1930
FAIRPLAY
ALMA
ALL MINES
IN THIS
DISTRICT

Atop the concrete block is a bronze plaque with a portrait of Prunes, and the monument is set with specimens of ore from all the mines in which the burro had worked. Prunes's skeleton was retrieved from the dump and buried behind the marker.

Sherwood died about a year after Prunes, on August 23, 1931, at the age of eighty-one. His last words were: "Bury me with Prunes." And so he was.

This would be the end of the story if not for a disturbing side note. In December of 1969, *The Golden* (Colo.) *Transcript* published a page-one article disclosing what it called "the hoax of Prunes the burro." According to this story, the "legend" of Prunes was simply the brainstorm of Sherwood and other miners who wanted to attract tourists to the struggling town of Fairplay. Basing his piece on interviews with old-timers who claimed to have known Prunes and Sherwood personally, the reporter wrote:

> Rube [Sherwood] never owned Prunes, never worked him, and probably couldn't have pointed him out in a group.... Probably the most unlikely aspect of the legend is the age ascribed to the jack. Burros are notably long-lived, but it is doubtful that any ever lived to the ripe old age of sixty-three, particularly if they spent the majority of those years tramming ore from underground or hauling ore and supplies in a pack train.
>
> One must remember that miners in those days worked hard, and played even harder. They had to devise their own entertainment. So it isn't surprising that they pulled many shenanigans on the gullible greenhorn and

hangers-on. But as some old-timers insist, the hoax of Prunes and Rube Sherwood may have "loused up" a bit of Colorado history, yet it didn't hurt anyone.

Who knows what to believe after so much time has passed, but it's tempting to accept that the legend is true. After all, no one disputes that there *was* a burro named Prunes or that it roamed the towns of Fairplay and Alma begging for food. And Prunes's monument *does* acknowledge an important part of Colorado history.

Joanna Stout, a Fairplay teacher and historian, admits that the story of Prunes "is probably pretty romanticized.

"There are a few cynics in town who believe it's a total hoax," she said, "but I think most everybody in town has just about accepted the story as is—because they like it."

When Stout tells the tale during "ghost tours" she leads around town, she calls it "factual and fictual," because she said she's "not sure where one starts and the other ends."

Despite the doubt, one must admit that the story of Prunes is charming and harmless. And besides, it's heart-warming to think that genuine devotion lay behind a poem Sherwood wrote in honor of the little burro—a poem he tearfully read at the dedication of Prunes's memorial. Titled "Me and Prunes," it runs ninety-two lines and reads in part:

> So poor old Prunes has cashed in. Too bad.
>   Still in a way
> I'm glad the old boy's eased off and calling it
>   a day.

I'm going to miss him scand'lous! The world
 won't seem the same
Not having him a'standing here hee-hawing
 in the game....

For Prunes was faithful, honest, an' he never
 tried to shirk
From doing his bit no matter how damned
 hard he worked,
And didn't grouch and grumble when the
 eats was kinda short.
He took all things just as they came. Old
 Prunes was a good sport!...

But I'm a gamblin' if there be another life
 after this one
It won't be just restricted to the things called
 man alone,
But everything now living will surely live
 again—
I know a hundred that deserves to, more
 than most of men.
An' if they do, why, shure as shootin'
 'mongst those heavenly tunes
I'll betcha fifty bucks we'll hear the hee-haw
 of old Prunes.

94

BUM AND SHORTY

INSEPARABLE PALS

*"The poor dog, in life the firmest friend,
The first to welcome, foremost to defend."*

Lord Byron
1808

The people of Fairplay have a soft spot in their hearts for burros, because Prunes isn't the only one to have inspired a monument in this sleepy mountain town. At the southwestern corner of the courthouse lawn sits another memorial: a granite tribute to the devotion between a burro known as Shorty and a mongrel dog called Bum.

This strange alliance began on a cold starry night in the fall of 1949, when Bum discovered Shorty drowsing in a pasture at the edge of town. Homeless and shivering, the short-haired mutt nestled up against the shaggy burro, and they kept each other warm for the remainder of the night. From then on, they were constant companions.

Like Prunes, Shorty had worked in the mines around Fairplay since his birth in 1906 at a small gold mine in Mosquito Gulch. Although he had unusually short legs—hence the name—the burro didn't seem to mind hauling heavy sacks of ore to the mills and dragging lumber to the mines to build the shafts. He worked at the South London and High Twelve mines and for several different owners until the Fairplay district began to peter out in the 1930s and 1940s. Shorty's last owner was one of the many miners who left to seek a new life elsewhere. No longer in need of a burro, he simply left Shorty behind.

For many years, the sturdy animal fended for itself, living off the lush grass that grew on nearby hillsides. But as it aged, its eyesight began to fail, and it had trouble foraging for food.

It was about this time that folks noticed a scrawny stray dog roaming the streets of Fairplay. Its build and coloration suggested it was part Dalmation, but the rest of its pedigree was indecipherable. As so often happens, it won the affection of two children who begged to make it their pet. They named it Bum because it had "bummed" its way into their home, and they gave it all the loving attention that every pet deserves.

Their father, however, didn't like dogs. Sometimes he kicked Bum or pelted him with sticks of firewood. Finally, the poor mutt could tolerate the cruelty no more. He fled the house and went back to his vagrant ways.

Bum's encounter with Shorty was serendipitous. He seemed to realize that the aging burro couldn't see, and he willingly assumed the role of seeing-eye dog. Every morning and evening, he led his new friend from door to door to beg for food, with Shorty following his scent.

The Denver Post once described their extraordinary ritual.

> Folks noticed that often the dog would go to a door, scratch and whine until food was offered. He then would pick up a choice bit, carry it to Shorty, standing a few paces away, and drop it at the burro's feet—as if to say "Look, pal, try this morsel I brought you!..."
>
> When the food was slow in coming Shorty would sound off with a loud bray, while Bum would stand by the kitchen door, head cocked to one side, ears erect and bright eyes looking expectantly for the door to open.

The pair's rounds grew so predictable that people often had a plate of leftovers ready when they came. The cook at the Hand Hotel even went a step further. She tossed Bum and Shorty warm pancakes and biscuits taken right off the platter that was about to be served to the paying guests.

When winter arrived, the two animals made the fortunate acquaintance of Johnnie Capelli, the courthouse janitor. He realized that they needed shelter from the bitter cold, so he made a bed of hay for them in his garage and parked his car outside. One particularly cold night, he smuggled them into the heated courthouse and let them sleep in the jail. He had to come to work early the next morning to free the inmates and clean out the cell before the sheriff showed up.

The seasons passed, and life was fairly easy for Bum and Shorty. They made many friends among the townspeople, and they were often met with smiles as they ambled down the sidewalks.

One late spring morning, the odd couple were making their early breakfast rounds when a chipmunk darted across a vacant lot on the opposite side of the street. Driven by instinct, Bum scrambled after it and was soon absorbed in the thrill of the chase. Shorty, of course, didn't realize that his buddy was only momentarily diverted. He stepped off the curb to follow Bum across the street—just as a car hurtled around the corner. It hit the burro and raced away, leaving him broken and bleeding in the gutter. Shorty died before anyone could come to his aid.

Not sure what else to do with it, someone loaded the burro's lifeless body into a wagon and hauled it to the town dump. For the next day or two, folks missed the regular visits of that inseparable pair. Even Bum seemed to have disappeared.

It was Capelli who finally realized where the dog must be. He drove out to the dump and found him keeping a lonely vigil at Shorty's side. When the janitor tried to coax Bum into his truck, the dog growled at him and refused to budge. Nothing, it seemed, could persuade Bum to abandon his best friend.

Finally, Capelli tried to convince the city marshal to bury Shorty, but the officer refused to use taxpayer money that way and offered to burn the carcass instead. The janitor went back to the dump and succeeded this time in getting a rope around Bum's neck. He took the mournful dog home with him and locked it in the garage until the cremation was over.

The people of Fairplay were touched by the bond between the blind burro and his devoted friend. They took up a collection and raised enough money to erect a monument etched with their likenesses. It read simply:

"SHORTY"
AGE 45 years - 1951
"BUM"
1949 -
"HIS BELOVED PAL"

Shorty's ashes were buried beside the monument, and folks planned to lay Bum to rest there, too, when the time came.

And the time came all too soon. One summer day, only weeks after Shorty's death, Bum stood on the courthouse lawn, waiting for a semi-trailer truck to pass by so he could cross the street. One account suggests that, in his grief, he may have wanted to die, and so he didn't dodge as quickly as he could have. Another speculated that he just didn't realize the length of the trailer. Whatever the reason, Bum trotted into the street too soon, and the great dual wheels of the rear axle struck and killed him.

Bum was buried at Shorty's side. And there the pair remain today—inseparable in death as they were in life.

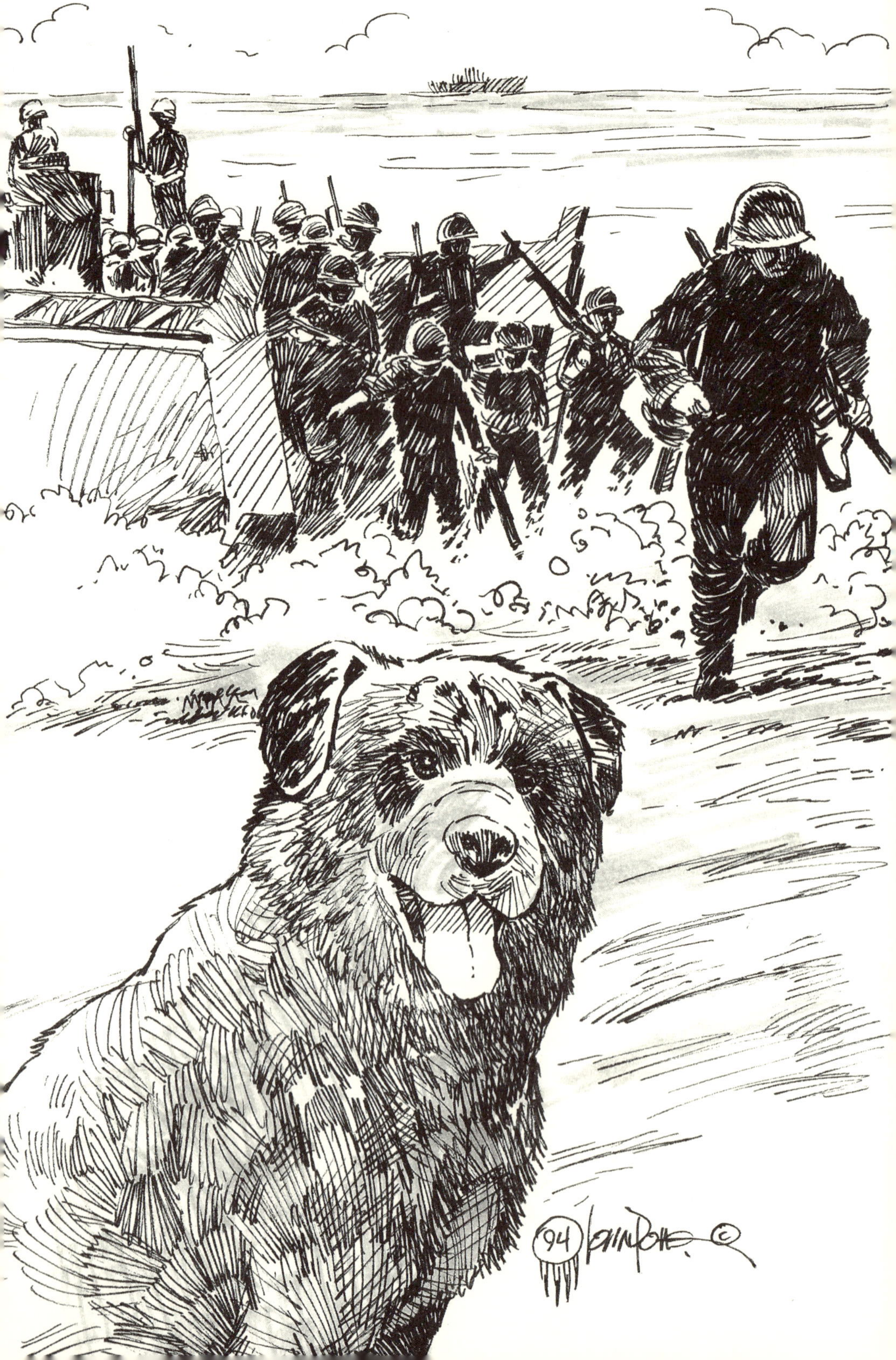

SKIPPER
WAR VETERAN

"Nature endowed this animal with his chief military value—an extraordinary development of the senses of smell and hearing.... These gifts, combined with [the] dog's unquestioning faithfulness, intelligence, adaptability, endurance, and utter willingness to serve for no more than a friendly pat and a kind word, have made him an important adjunct in man's wars down through the ages."

Clayton G. Going
Dogs at War

On July 10, 1943, thousands of British and American troops crammed themselves into landing craft, bucked a choppy sea, and swarmed onto the beaches of southern Sicily. For thirty-eight days, they grappled their way across the island, pushing back German and Italian forces that blew up bridges and mined roads to cover their retreat. More than 150,000 enemy soldiers and 19,000 Allies were killed or wounded during the massive invasion. One of them—an American GI known as Skipper—lost a leg in a mine explosion. For the rest of his life, he would have to gimp around on only three.

Obviously, Skipper was no ordinary soldier. Part chow and part bulldog, he was a member of the K-9 Corps, an elite force that helped ensure an Allied victory in World War II. He was trained to sniff out land mines, and his talent saved the lives of countless soldiers during the North African campaign as well as the invasion of Sicily. He won nine battle stars and a Purple Heart, according to one report.

After the war, Skipper found a home with another veteran, Ray Denny, a Denver man who had served in the Navy. Both dog and master joined Littleton Post 4666, Veterans of Foreign Wars, and together they marched in VFW parades, with Skipper decked out in his own special uniform.

Skipper never let his war handicap interfere with his enjoyment of civilian life. In 1951, eight years after his honorable discharge, *The Denver Post* reported that

> Skipper has two bad habits, one of them a carryover from his service training. He just can't resist digging holes all over the lawn, perhaps still imagining he is digging mines. The other bad habit is chasing motorcycles—and in this, too, he doesn't seem to be hampered much by the loss of his front leg.

That man should draft dogs to serve beside him in battle shouldn't be too surprising; it's been happening for ages. Ancient Egyptian wall paintings, believed to date back as far as 4,000 B.C., show savage dogs leaping at the throats of enemy soldiers and straining against leashes held by Egyptian warriors. The Spanish conquistadores used attack dogs to help them conquer Mexico and Peru. The Gauls even dressed their war dogs in armor, including heavy iron collars from which spikes and knives protruded. Dogs served with Attila the Hun, with Napoleon, and with Admiral Collingwood at the Battle of Trafalgar.

The first American war dogs belonged to the Indians, whose barking sentries alerted sleeping camps to the approach of enemy warriors. Then, in 1775, Benjamin Franklin proposed turning the tables. He suggested using scout dogs to defend against Indian raids. The accomplished statesman, author, and scientist recommended that the dogs

> ...should be large, strong and fierce; and every dog led in a slip string, to prevent their tiring themselves by running out and in, and [revealing the location of] the party by barking at squirrels, etc. Only when the party come near thick woods and suspicious places they should turn out a dog or two to search them. In case of meeting a party of the enemy, the dogs are all then to be turned loose and set on.

Nothing came of Franklin's idea. In fact, his countrymen never did employ war dogs in any organized way until World War II—even though, in World War I, the Germans and their allies unleashed as many as 75,000 of them.

By the time the Japanese attacked Pearl Harbor in 1941, Germany had trained an estimated 200,000 sentry, scout, and messenger dogs and had supplied Japan with 25,000. The French, British, and Russians had also begun deploying canine troops.

The impetus to draft U.S. dogs came from an unexpected quarter: the nation's pooch-loving public. Within hours of Pearl Harbor, a dog fancier named Mrs. Milton S. Erlanger phoned a New York newspaperman and issued the call to arms.

"The dog world must play its part in this thing," she told him. "Other countries have used dogs in their armies for years and ours has not. We've got to do it!"

The end result of the call was that dog breeders, trainers, and handlers; kennel club members; show judges; and veterinarians—in short, people who owned dogs and loved them—got together to form a volunteer organization called Dogs for Defense. Their first challenge was to convince the U.S. military that dogs could put more teeth into the war effort.

They started by training sentry dogs to guard munitions plants, oil fields, and supply depots on the home front. It soon became obvious that the dog's superior senses of hearing and smell were immensely valuable, especially during nighttime blackouts when a soldier's vision was limited. The presence of a dog companion also tremendously boosted the morale of soldiers assigned to lonely sentry duty.

In March 1942, the Army demonstrated that it *is* possible to teach an old dog new tricks. It finally agreed to try using two hundred sentry dogs for defense purposes. Out of this modest order would grow a canine army of close to 20,000. Called WAGS at first, the four-legged soldiers soon became known as the K-9 Corps. They worked as sentries, defending military installations against spies and saboteurs; as scouts, alerting troops to snipers and enemy ambushes; and as messengers, carrying dispatches over dangerous terrain when other lines of communication were broken. They served as mine detectors, locating deadly mines and booby traps so soldiers could avoid them; as sledge dogs, rescuing airmen downed in the snowy Arctic; and as casualty dogs, finding wounded soldiers hidden from view on battlefields or buried in bombing debris. They fought and died beside servicemen from the Army, Marines, and Coast Guard.

For the sake of consistency and efficiency, the military decided to handle the training of its canine corps itself. It gave Dogs for Defense the responsibility of recruiting the animals, and this the group did by initiating a grass-roots publicity campaign that played on the patriotism of dog owners nationwide. Through speeches and the print and broadcast media, members of the organization did their best to convince people of the great service their dogs could perform.

Americans were asked to donate their dogs unconditionally and with no guarantee that their pets would ever be returned. The U.S. Government issued certificates of gratitude to the owners, but, as one author pointed out, "their real recompense, of course, was the knowledge that they had performed an act of patriotism, an act the more deeply patriotic as it meant the sacrifice of something cherished."

Hundreds of people—rich and poor, city and country, distinguished and undistinguished—volunteered to enlist their pets. For some, the offer probably meant good riddance, but for most, the decision was heartrending. Dogs for Defense received mailbags full of poignant letters, like this one from a California boy:

> I am eight years old and live on a farm. I have a large Australian Shepherd dog about two and one-half years old that is a very good hunter and I think he would be good hunting [the enemy]. He sure likes to kill skunks.... If you

need a real good dog, I will loan you mine until the war is over.

To be eligible for service, a dog had to be between the ages of one and five, more than twenty inches tall at the shoulder, at least fifty pounds in weight, and in good physical condition. It also had to be alert, somewhat aggressive, and unintimidated by loud explosions. Females as well as males were acceptable, and purebreds were preferred.

Folks whose animals were unsuitable for service could enroll them in a sort of K-9 home guard instead. All a person had to do was contribute money to the Dogs for Defense War Dog Fund, and in return he would receive a certificate assigning his pet an honorary military rank. For a dollar, Fido could become a private or seaman, while $100 would make him general or admiral of his own domain. Even President Roosevelt enlisted his Scottie dog, Fala. Others made contributions in the name of cats, birds, and turtles.

Once the K-9 program was under way, Dogs for Defense was hounded by men, women, and children wanting to know how Private Rover was getting along. Military regulations prohibited the group from answering these queries once the dog in question had been transferred to active duty. Nor could donors visit the training centers to see their former pets. One lucky mistress accidentally got around this restriction when she attended an exhibition of war-dog training. The unexpected reunion was described in *Dogs for Defense*, by Fairfax Downey.

A spectator... suddenly recognized her own contribution to the K-9's in the group which trainers were putting through their paces. Proud of her pet's performance, the woman owner could not resist telling the officer in charge. The officer, forming a sudden resolution, invited her to enter the ring. From across the arena the dog caught sight of his mistress. Ears pricked up, eyes shone with recognition, tail began thumping on the ground.

"Stay," the dog's handler commanded. At the officer's urging, the woman called her dog by name. The dog sat like a statue and never stirred, only quivering a little. His handler, proud too now, bent his head toward his charge and said softly, "Okay." With that the dog darted away, racing across the ring in great bounds. With one of those unmelodious but poignant canine cries of joy a dog sometimes utters, he sprang into his mistress' arms, licking her face with loving tongue. Yet when his handler called him back, he instantly obeyed. The Army could not have asked for a more striking example of perfect discipline and training.

K-9 basic training would have been the envy of every two-legged soldier. Each dog was well-fed, issued its own clean, comfortable kennel, and given days or even weeks to become used to its surroundings before getting down to business. Then, for anywhere from two weeks to three months, the recruits attended class for just a few hours a day to learn the fundamentals—heel, sit, stay, come, and so on. They also were taught to wear gas masks and muzzles and to endure the sound of heavy-caliber gunfire and land-mine explosions.

Ironically, members of the K-9 Corps were the only U.S. soldiers *not* issued dog tags. Instead, a serial number was tattooed on the inside of the left ear.

If a recruit successfully completed basic training, it went on to specialize. Danny, a German shepherd donated by a Denver resident, became a sentry dog. He had the chance to prove himself after less than a month on duty. While patrolling the U.S. Army Air Forces school at Stuttgart, Arkansas, he discovered a fire in the lumberyard, and his warning saved Uncle Sam many board feet of valuable timber.

The combination of man's best friend and man's meanest enterprise was guaranteed to produce countless tales of loyalty, bravery, intelligence, and stamina. The stories of Skipper and Danny are but two of them. No one knows how many Coloradans sacrificed their pets for the good of their country, and no one will ever know how many lives were saved as a result.

Writing in 1943, Thomas Yoseloff may have best summed up the worthy contributions of Skipper and his fellow K-9s in his book *Dogs for Democracy*.

> There is a story behind each record of America's canine heroes—a story that is sentimental or dramatic, humorous or pathetic. And when we have won again our right to live the American way of life, our dog-army will have shared in the battle, and have won the right to a share in the glory.

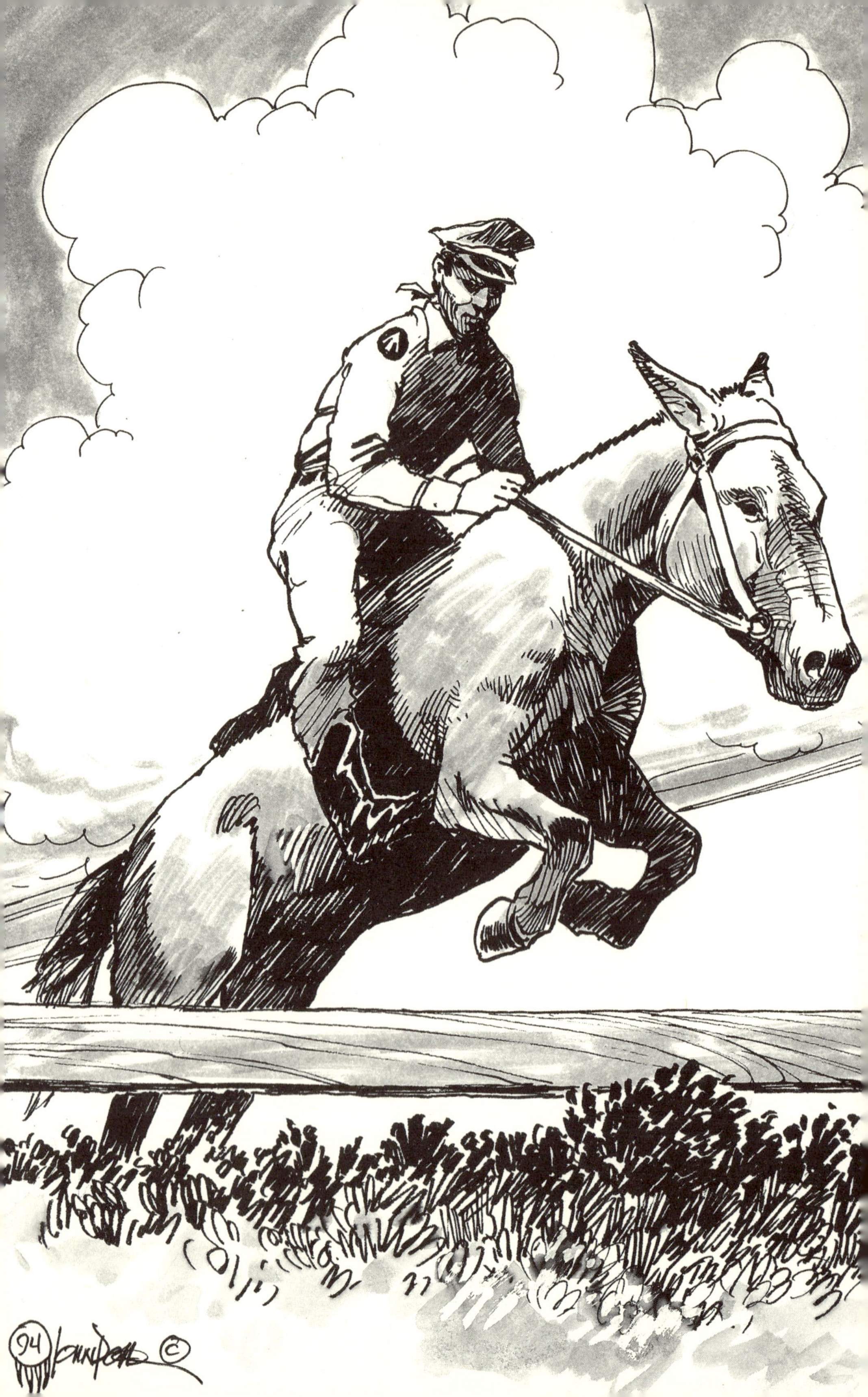

HAMBONE

JUMPIN' FOOL

"The Army's mules are dead—except for a memory stuck with muley affection in the minds of tough men who once shared a life with them."

Columbus Smith
The Sun, Colorado Springs, Colo.
April 17, 1971

The commander at Fort Carson saluted smartly as more than three hundred soldiers—two-legged and four-legged—passed in review for the last time. The mountains west of the sprawling army base wore caps of snow on that historic Saturday, December 15, 1956. Bright banners slapped at the breeze, and the frosty breath of the army pack mules and their human handlers clouded the air as they marched into retirement. There, on the high plains of central Colorado, a colorful era was drawing to a close. From now on, helicopters, not mules, would transport equipment for the U.S. Army.

Among the spectators in the reviewing stand that day were a pair of specially invited guests. Hambone and Trotter couldn't have understood the significance of this stirring ceremony and the distinction that was about to be bestowed upon them. No doubt they just waggled their long ears, shifted their weight from hip to hip, and dreamed of endless fields of hay.

But as the colors of the pack-mule units were retired forever, Hambone and Trotter were led before Major General Harry P. Storke and presented with citations for outstanding service. Trotter's certificate read in part:

> Your long and devoted service has included two round-trip overland tours of the 190-mile distance to Cheyenne, Wyoming, and four round-trip tours to Camp Hale, 150 miles distant, as well as participation in all exercises conducted at Camp Hale since 1949. Special recognition is also made of your exceptional abilities in that you are the single one out of thousands [of mules] who is master of four gaits: the walk, trot, gallop, and pace.
>
> The presentation of this certificate on the occasion of the deactivation of the Army mules is accompanied by the firm hope that your retirement will not be plagued with those horrors which, in times past, have caused you to unburden yourself rather hurriedly of riders and other equipment—a glimpse of either of those hideous devices, the umbrella or the bicycle.

Then it was Hambone's turn for recognition. General Storke cleared his throat, planted his tongue in his other cheek, and told the world of the mule's achievements.

Your long, devoted and well-publicized service has included maneuvers during three winters at Camp Hale and two round trips to Cheyenne, Wyoming, the last of which was made entirely overland during the summer of 1956.

Special commendation is due to you for your extraordinary abilities displayed in jumping events, and for the record of having never lost a mule jumping contest, as well as for your phenomenal success in bettering all except the first place winner in a competition with horses at Fort Carson in 1950.

In addition, your exhibition jumping at the International Stock Show in Chicago in 1950, at the Pikes Peak Rodeo in 1954, and at other equestrian functions has been a credit both to yourself and the Army.

Back in the reviewing stand, the two mules watched as an army helicopter hovered into view and dipped its fuselage in salute. Thus, in a whirlwind of dust, the aircraft paid homage to the thousands of mules that had served the U.S. war effort—and at the same time accepted the responsibility of carrying on the pack animals' mission.

Now that his career as a beast of burden was over, Trotter was appointed mascot of the West Point military academy, a cushy job he held from 1957 to 1972. He died at a New York farm in December 1981 at the age of fifty-one.

Hambone, however, went on to become a Colorado celebrity.

Hamilton T. Bone—Hambone for short—had been foaled in May 1932 on a farm in Missouri. Like every mule, he had a perfectly respectable mare for a mother. But his father—let's face it—was a jackass.

Despite such plebian ancestry, it became obvious early on that Hambone was not your average mule. For one thing, he was white instead of the usual black and brown. For another, as it turned out, he could outjump many a fine thoroughbred horse—a surprising skill for a lowly mule.

Hambone joined the Army about 1940, when a tough sergeant bought him for $210 at St. Joseph, Missouri. He was stationed at Forts Reno, Sill, and Riley before making his home at Fort Carson in 1946.

The U.S. military had long known the advantages of using mules for draft, riding, and pack purposes. They were more rugged than horses, had more stamina and stability, and could subsist on inferior rations. Even George Washington experimented with them, and a Civil War general once remarked, "The Civil War could not have been carried to a conclusion without the mule."

In his book *Animal Reveille*, Richard Dempewolff couldn't praise mules enough.

> The mule's flinty feet, inborn caution, and patience make him ideal for traversing precipices, stony roads, and jungles where wheeled transport cannot penetrate. As early as 1940 the U.S. Army discovered that its supermachines were fine and speedy in open country. But when it came to mud, jungles, mountain trails, and cowpaths, four sturdy legs still made the best time. North African rains

stopped everything but the mules; Philippine mountains gave them a chance to show off their goat-like characteristics; they served bravely through the slaughter of Bataan—and then, at the last, they provided meat for troops that had been cut off from supplies.

Mules did, however, require special handling "in order to get the best out of them," Dempewolff pointed out. According to army men, he said, "they must be roundly cussed at frequent intervals... because the animals are used to being called dirty names—and resent it if their pranks don't get a rise out of their masters."

Hambone apparently was no exception. An "old-timer" was once quoted as saying he remembered the mule "driving his handlers nutty." He said it "took pounds of spit and sweat and a ton of cussing to turn him into a first-rate mule."

According to an article in *The Denver Post*, Hambone served two combat missions overseas during World War II, one of which took him to Germany. He then reportedly did a stint in Hollywood where he made three movies.

No one could accuse Hambone of not pulling—or at least carrying—his weight in the army. Six days a week, he hauled weapon parts weighing as much as three hundred pounds during forced marches into the mountains with the Fourth Field Artillery Battalion stationed at Fort Carson. Once he even climbed Pikes Peak with a heavy howitzer part strapped to his back. It took two men to remove his load.

Life in the army wasn't easy for the "muleskinners," either. One of them ruefully recalled his role in the field exercises.

> Normally in an infantry unit you take a ten minute break, lay down in the shade and watch the world go by, but not in the mule pack.
>
> You adjust the loads, crack cinches to let them breathe, watch for cinch burns, wither burns, adjust all the rigging, and just when you thought you would take a breather they say "Move out...."

Muleskinning required talent as well as endurance. As one soldier put it, "They used to say you were a mule packer when you could pack a baby grand piano on one side of the pack and a box of matches on the other side and balance the load."

It was what Hambone did on his day off each week that won him national fame. Early in his military career, while he was stationed at Fort Riley, Kansas, his handler entered him in a horse show. He won the jumping events "hooves down," but when the judges found out they'd been bamboozled by a mule, they made him return his ribbons.

In 1948, after his transfer to Colorado, Hambone "embarrassed the horsy set half to death" by winning the jumper classic of the Camp Carson Hunt Club. The next year, the club refused to let him compete, and this caught the attention of *Life* magazine. "Mule Beats Horses," an article in the July issue reported. "Barred From Competition With His Social Betters, He Is Still Army's Best Jumper at Camp Carson." The story was accompanied by five photographs of Hambone in action.

When the pack mule units were abolished in 1956, the army sold Hambone to Jasper D. Ackerman of the

Pikes Peak or Bust Rodeo. For the next fourteen years, the aging animal was a regular feature of the rodeos held each year in Colorado Springs, and he took part in the annual one-hundred-mile Pikes Peak Range Ride as well.

Finally, at the age of thirty, Hambone was turned out to pasture for good. He died March 29, 1971, of congestive heart failure and was buried with appropriate military honors in front of the Fourth Infantry Division Artillery headquarters at Fort Carson. A stone memorial was erected over his grave.

During Hambone's heydey, a serviceman stationed at Castle Air Force Base in California had heard of his exploits and written a song about the "jumpin' fool." When he learned of Hambone's death, he added a new verse:

> Now Hambone loved the Army,
> The Army loved him, too;
> We all wish Hambone's happy
> Where mules go when they're through.

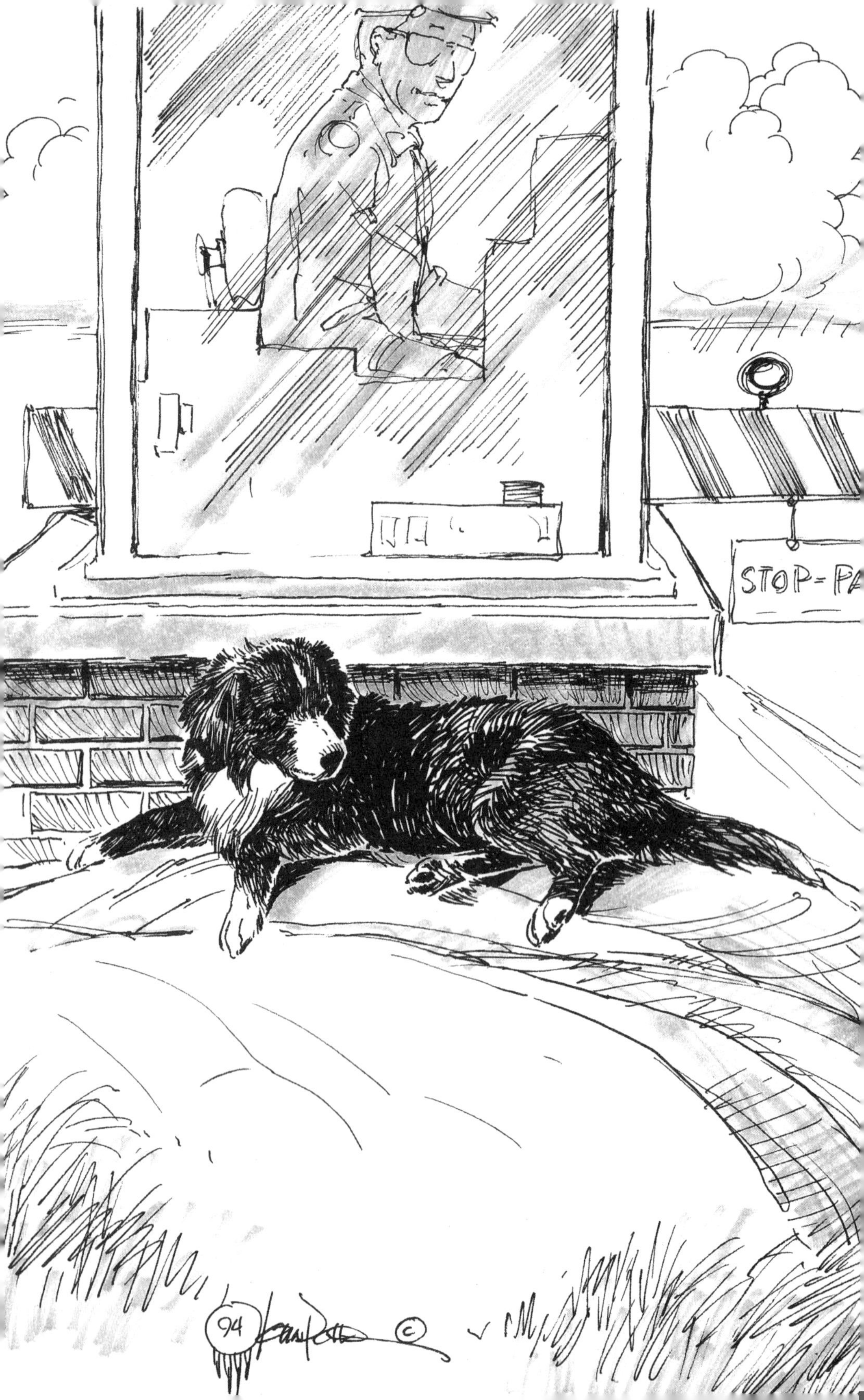
STOP-PA

SHEP
TURNPIKE MASCOT

"People may forget about the dog who brightened the lives of so many, [but] his grave will always remain as a symbol of the love that people have for animals."

The Citizen
October 1989

A gaggle of grinning politicians posed for the photographers. They delivered the usual gushy speeches strewn with quotable catchwords. Finally, they broke the tape to open the new multimillion-dollar highway that would link two sister cities on the Colorado Front Range.

About five thousand people turned out for the dedication of the Denver-Boulder Turnpike on that Saturday, January 19, 1952. Somewhere in that throng stood a shaggy black and white mongrel, and it probably didn't appreciate this invasion of the place that it called home.

No one knows exactly where the dog came from. It showed up one day in 1951 when the seventeen-mile toll road was still under construction. A timid pup, it lived off scraps of sandwiches the workers tossed its way, and it came and went with all the freedom of a carefree bachelor. When the highway was completed, it adopted the tollhouse at the Broomfield interchange, midway between Boulder and Denver, as its home. Since it appeared to be part shepherd, employees there named it Shep.

At first, Shep was a little wary of the men whose job it was to collect quarters from vacationers and commuters.

"He would come a little closer every day," recalled Leander "Ole" Bruhn, who worked at the tollbooth for almost seventeen years. "He'd follow the boys [toll collectors] after a while, but when they turned around, he'd run. It was sort of a pathetic thing."

But patience and kindness paid off. On an especially frigid evening in the winter of 1953, Shep allowed himself to be coaxed into the tollbooth for a warm night's sleep. For the next eleven years, he served as the gatekeepers' pet, running to greet their cars at the beginning of every shift. He became a fixture to the thousands of travelers who passed through the tollgate each year.

"Every day, he'd sit there on the concrete buffer and watch people go by," Bruhn said. "When he wasn't there, people would always ask for him."

In fact, the unassuming stray became something of a celebrity. Folks would hand the collectors more than the required quarter and tell them to "keep the change for Shep." Vacationers on annual trips to Colorado would bring along toys for the dog. One Boulder couple sent the collectors a check for dog food every Christmas.

Shep even had a friend or two in high places.

"I was working there one day," one gatekeeper remembered with a chuckle, "when this man in a station wagon paid his toll, then got out and put a case of dog food on the top of the wall. He handed me his card. 'When you run out of that,' he told me, 'give me a call, and I'll bring you some more.' He was a salesman for a dog-food company."

Shep managed to shake a free lunch out of the Highway Patrol now and then, too.

"He'd jump right in their cars when they stopped at the booth," one collector said. "They'd take him in to Boulder for a hamburger and then bring him back."

Eventually, the story of Shep spread nationwide, and the toll collectors began to get cards and letters from all over, asking after his welfare. Some people tucked a five- or ten-dollar bill in with their correspondence.

Still, life at the tollbooth wasn't just a bowl of Alpo. Once, Shep tangled with a pack of coyotes and wound up on the bottom of the heap. A sympathetic Broomfield veterinarian patched him up free of charge. In September 1958, someone peppered the dog with shotgun pellets with the excuse that he'd been chasing sheep. The same vet put a cast on his shattered left foreleg. In November 1961, the vet removed a tumor from Shep's right eyelid.

"He was such a nice dog," the vet, Dr. Clyde Brunner, once explained, "and he sort of became a shared responsibility of the people in the booth, drivers, and myself. He lived a good life, and everyone who knew him loved him."

Shep may not have been afraid to tackle a gang of coyotes, but he had a healthy respect for motor vehicles (and a downright hatred of telephone trucks). Perhaps the most surprising thing about his residence at the tollbooth is that he never once was hit by a car—even though he trotted back and forth across the highway several times a day.

But no dog can cheat death forever. By the summer of 1964, Shep was an estimated fifteen or sixteen years old—elderly for a canine. He was blind, deaf, and limping with arthritis, and the toll collectors had to carry him out of the booth at the start of each day. Dr. Brunner reluctantly recommended that Shep be put to sleep, and on August 3 the tollhouse pet breathed his last. It's easy to picture him greeting travelers on that heavenly road as it passes through the pearly gates.

The story doesn't end there. The toll collectors wouldn't let it. They buried Shep in a triangle of grass between the on and off ramps at the Broomfield interchange and pooled their money to buy a white marble headstone inset with the dog's picture. On it is this inscription: "Shep, 1950-1964, Partly Shepherd, Mostly Affection."

Today, the grave still overlooks the intersection of U.S. 36 and Colorado 121. A knee-high, wrought-iron fence surrounds it, and a solitary tree shrouds it in shade.

A month after Shep's death, a dog-loving Colorado artist painted a portrait of the turnpike mascot and presented it to the toll collectors. For years it hung in the tollhouse, a tangible reminder of a loving pet. When the booth closed in 1967, the picture was moved to the main office of the state Department of Transportation in Denver, and it hangs there still.

To the end of their days, the men who staffed the tollbooth of the Denver-Boulder Turnpike will fondly keep Shep's memory alive. In a 1981 interview with the

Rocky Mountain News, Bruhn expressed just one regret about his days with the devoted dog.

"We never did train him," he said, "and we should have because he was so smart. But if we had, I would have taught him to stand out in front of the booth with a basket in his mouth so he could catch the coins the people threw. They would've gotten the biggest kick out of that."

It's a likely bet that Shep would have, too.

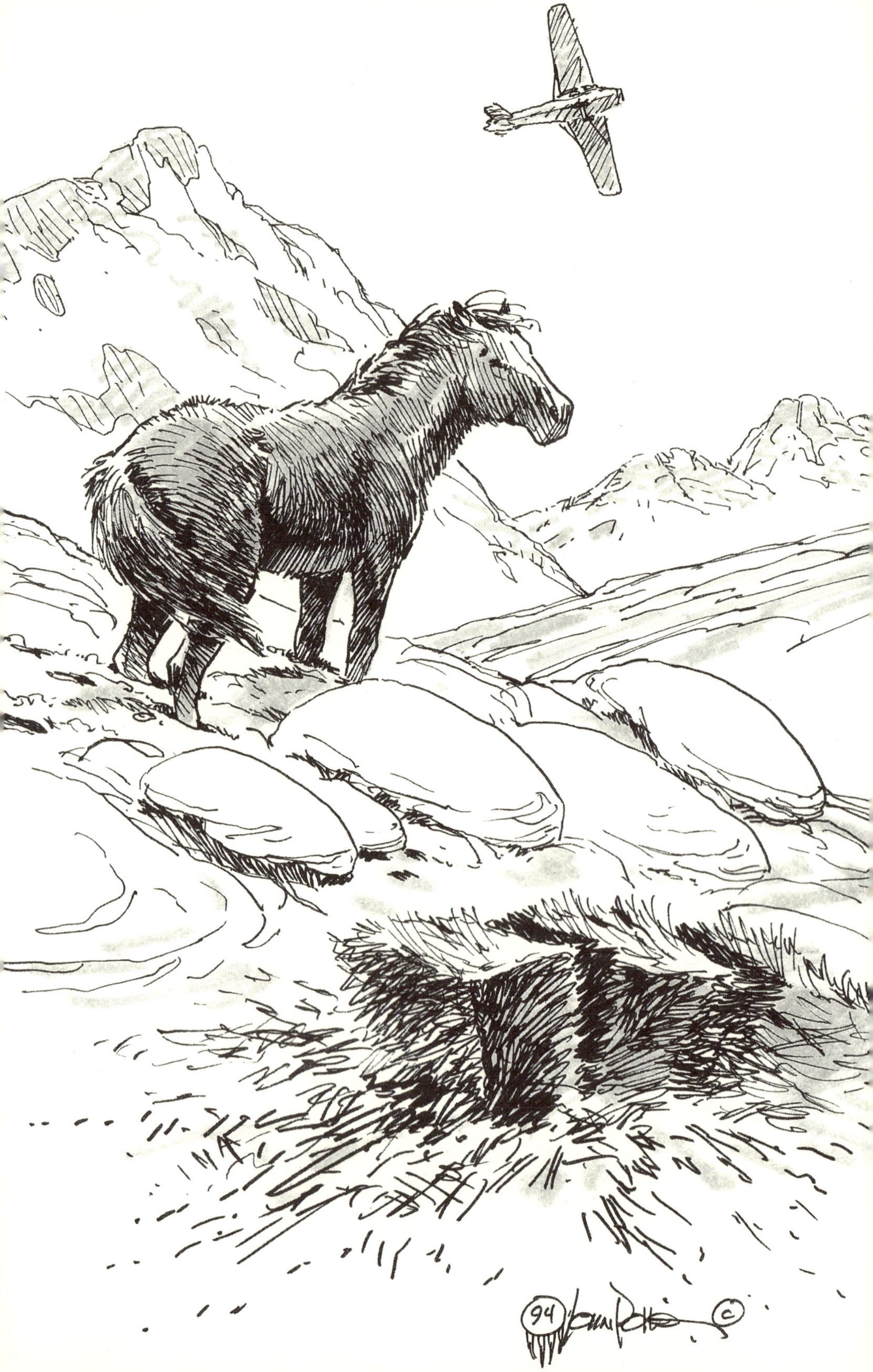
94

ELIJAH
HARRIED HERMIT

"Do-gooders are a wonderful people, and we all love their kind hearts, bless 'em. But they can be an awful nuisance, too, if the object of their good deeds seeks nothing more than being left to his own private devices."

Editorial
The Denver Post
April 11, 1956

On a brittle-cold day in February 1956, Wallace Powell's single-engine airplane bucked its way over the Continental Divide. Down below, the skyscrapers of central Colorado's Collegiate Range—peaks stretching higher than 14,000 feet—wore slickers of blinding snow. Not even a tree could survive at this altitude, especially in this weather, so Powell wasn't expecting to see signs of life.

But wait! What were those dark specks moving across the bleak, 13,000-foot saddle that links mounts Yale and Harvard?

Could they be.... No, that was impossible! They were horses—one gray, one bay, both standing forlornly with their tails to the bitter wind.

Powell was troubled. He didn't know how or when the animals had reached the shelterless ridge, but he knew the deep snow must have trapped them there. They would starve to death long before the June thaw set them free.

When Powell touched down in Gunnison, about forty miles southwest of the ridge, he told Gordon Warren, his boss at Western State Aviation Service, about the stranded horses. Together, they reported the predicament to the mayor, Ben Jorgensen, who had served as a volunteer officer of the state Humane Association for many years. So not surprisingly he was a sucker for animals in distress. He offered to cover the cost if the pilots would drop two bales of hay onto the ridge each week—$12 a bale including the flight time.

And so began a dangerous mission of mercy that would capture the attention and sympathy of millions of people around the world.

When Warren dropped the first of the manna from heaven, only one horse—the bay—was there on the ridge to welcome him. The other, he surmised, had died and lay buried under drifting snow. Warren released the hay as close to the gaunt survivor as he could, and when he flew away, the horse was munching happily.

From then on, Warren and Powell took turns flying the haylift. Soon they felt a personal responsibility for the pitiful prisoner of the wilderness.

"He's always waiting for us," Warren said. "When we make a pass to drop the first half-bale, he runs around and kicks up his heels. By the time we make the second pass, he's eating and doesn't even look up.

"We hated to disappoint that old boy," he later told a reporter. "Several times Wally and I flew up there when 100-mile gusts were bouncing our tiny plane all over the ridge. That horse was getting the kind of flying out of us that money can't buy."

In early April, Warren took some aerial photographs of the horse, and these made their way into the hands of George McWilliams, a reporter for *The Denver Post*. Sensing a good sob story, he called the pilot for details. For one thing, he wanted to know, did the horse have a name? An article in *The Reader's Digest* explained what happened next.

> "No," Warren replied. "If you can think of a good one you're welcome to tag it on him."
>
> McWilliams turned to a fellow reporter and said: "What was the name of that fellow in the Bible who was fed by ravens?"
>
> "Elijah [the prophet]," the reporter said.
>
> "That's the perfect name." McWilliams turned to his typewriter and hammered out the story of Elijah, the hermit horse.

For the rest of the month, the story of Elijah became a daily feature of the *Post*, often dominating the front page. Response to the initial story was prompt and overwhelming. Officers at the U.S. Army's Mountain Cold Weather Training Command at Camp Hale, Colorado, began studying the idea of using infantry troops to rescue the hapless horse. An American Airlines pilot bound from New York to Los Angeles asked for Elijah's precise location so he could point out the animal to his passengers. Officials at the Centennial Race Track on the outskirts of Denver started a fund with which to feed Elijah and kicked in the first $100 themselves. They also offered to stable and feed the horse if no one claimed him after his rescue, but dozens of children clamored for the chance to keep him, too. An eleven-year-old Lakewood girl wrote,

> If Elijah doesn't have an owner, I wish with all my heart I could have him when he is rescued. I have been wanting a horse all my life, but my mother can't afford to buy one for me. I would be very good to him. I plan on baby sitting and selling fishworms this summer to earn money to feed him.

Newspapers from coast to coast picked up Elijah's story, and he soon became "the most worried-about horse in the U.S.," according to *Life* magazine. Letters poured in from as far away as France, England, Portugal, Switzerland, Holland, Germany, Canada, and Japan. An American in Paris even suggested getting the United Nations involved:

> Couldn't the Post present this problem to the United Nations or Unesco which would be the logical means of reaching the heart and mind of the nations which belong to these organizations? It seems to me that the most essential requisite for mankind to possess is humanity and to know how to be kind to all animals and to put into practice that kindness.
> If it is naturally lacking in the human race then it requires an organization powerful enough to impose it and to teach mankind that peoples cruel to animals are also cruel to humans.

Meanwhile, in Buena Vista, Colorado, brothers Al and Bill Turner followed the ongoing saga of Elijah with more than passing interest. Outfitters by profession, they knew horses, and after carefully studying the aerial photos printed in the *Post*, they decided they knew this particular horse better than most. In a letter to Gunnison's Mayor Jorgensen, they claimed Elijah looked suspiciously like Bugs, a tough old packhorse they had lost—along with a gray horse named Smokey—the previous fall.

"If Elijah is Bugs," they continued, "he certainly knows the country better than any horse alive.... He hates parked cars and women in skirts, which would certainly be motive enough for heading for the high country."

The story of Elijah had suddenly taken "a chilling turn," as the *Post* editorial writer was quick to point out. Could all the hubbub over the hermit horse simply have been "a hideous invasion of privacy?" he asked.

> All the kind-hearted attention that has been lavished on Elijah is one thing; but if the horse is really Bugs, that's a horse of a different color.
>
> Bugs... could presumably get down from his mountain hide-away any time he wants to, which would be the way he got up. But if it is Bugs, it seems evident he doesn't want to come down.... If it is Bugs, leave him alone. He's minding his own business and using his good horse sense in seeking solitude.

But by now the *Post* had invested a lot of time and newsprint in its Save-A-Horse campaign. Readers were following the story as though it were a favorite soap opera. One of them, an Air Force veteran, had even offered to parachute onto the ridge and keep Elijah company until spring. How could the *Post* just drop the story now? It had manufactured a celebrity. Plans to rescue Elijah, regardless of his feelings in the matter, continued.

On the morning of April 11, a five-person *Post* rescue team led by Bill Turner donned snowshoes and made the seven-mile climb to Elijah's windswept hermitage. Although they weren't able to return with the horse in tow, they did bring back two important bits of information: Elijah was "fat and sassy," and he was most definitely Bugs. The *Post* reported that

> ...the Turners... called the horse to them, put a rope halter on him and fed him a bag of oats.... Bill Turner said he not only recognized Elijah as his horse Bugs, but found his brand—Heart Two Bar—on the horse's left shoulder. The Turners said they will try to bring the horse out some time in May when the deep snow has gone and will put him back to work. The one-horse haylift... will be continued.

Now that Elijah's well-being was assured, the *Post* began to receive a sprinkling of less charitable letters about its Save-A-Horse campaign. One Coloradan wrote:

> Why—when our poor world needs money, time and help from thoughtful people, when people are starving in our own country—why, in the name of everything that's good, do we waste our limited pity and sentiment on a pack

horse? Why do our newspapers so obviously encourage this misplaced sentiment?

Another letter-writer was even more blunt. "When theres people in Eurup an evin in United Stats starving it aint rite to make such a blam fuss over no horse. I say shoot him. You kin even borrey my 30-30."

In late May, the Turners tried again to retrieve their marooned horse. This time they were accompanied only by a Buena Vista wrangler who was selected, the Turners said, because "he's one heck of a shoveler." In some places, the men had to dig a path for Elijah through snowdrifts ten to twenty feet deep, working hours to progress only a few yards. Night caught them several miles short of the road, so they picketed the horse and returned to town. The next day, they loaded him into a trailer and drove him home to Buena Vista.

Until now, Elijah could have had no idea how famous he'd become, but when he rolled into Buena Vista, he was given a hero's welcome. The high school band led a parade down Main Street, followed by Elijah himself, a string of honking cars, and several floats, one of them depicting the hay delivery. More than a thousand people (the town's entire population plus a few hundred more) turned out to watch. Elijah's silent and solitary life was most definitely over.

And that was only the beginning. That same afternoon, Elijah was whisked to Denver for the opening of the quarterhorse racing season at the Centennial Track. Seven thousand people cheered as the bewildered bay stood in the winner's circle to receive a red and white blanket from the city mayor. Elijah went on to star in a Denver parade, and, of course, he made a brief stop at *The Denver Post* to meet his benefactors.

Six days after his rescue, Elijah got an even headier taste of the high life. He clopped his way up a strip of red carpet and checked into Denver's famous Brown Palace Hotel. "It seemed only natural that he join the roster of notables who have stayed at the hotel," the *Post* maintained.

Elijah was given a stall that had been specially prepared for him in one corner of the lobby. The management had, however, taken the precaution of laying a piece of heavy canvas under his bed of straw.

Alas, it soon became apparent that Elijah was beginning to tire of the lifestyle of the rich and famous. As the *Post* reported,

> Mrs. Nettie Shepard, a waitress, and John Cotsiomitis, a bellhop, showed Elijah a menu while movie and still cameras clicked and tape recorders ground out the story. Elijah pawed restlessly and pushed the waitress away with his nose.
>
> It was first planned to have the horse on view in the lobby all day. But he seemed so anxious to get away from it all that the Turner brothers led him back to the trailer and returned him to the track.

Life in the city was fraught with too many parked cars and women in skirts for Elijah's tastes.

After about two weeks of high living, Elijah went back to Buena Vista and his comparatively restful job carting fishermen and dudes into the Rockies. No doubt he soon forgot his fleeting brush with fame. No doubt the public soon forgot him and found other causes to ballyhoo. For the next fifteen years, Elijah avoided the public eye.

Then, in September 1971, Elijah's picture once again graced the pages of *The Denver Post*. Colorado's famous "horse on a mountain" had died at the age of twenty-seven—a merciful bullet in his brain. The obituary was a little late. Bill Turner had found him crippled and in poor condition the previous March and had put him out of his misery. Still, what the tribute lacked in timeliness it made up for in sentiment. It said:

> Although at one time he'd personified the rugged, unpampered western horse and had won the hearts of admirers in every country where the news is printed, there was no fancy funeral for Elijah—no monument—just the tall, treeless, silent mountain peaks. What more could a horse ask?

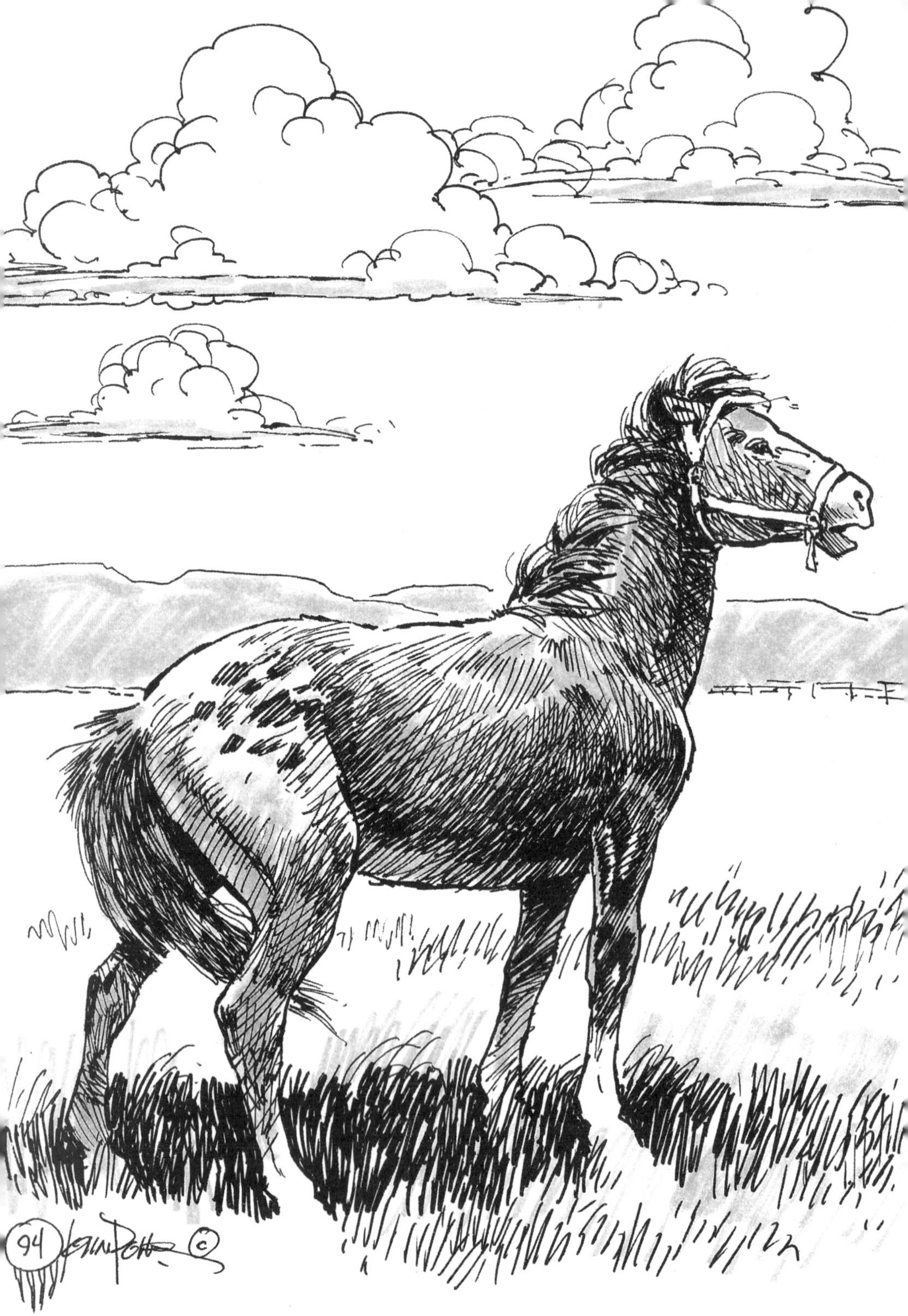

SNIPPY
HEADLESS HOAX?

> *"Attention, Martians (or whoever you may be)! If you came in your saucer to Earth, landed in the San Luis Valley and slew poor Snippy the horse, be advised that we Earthlings hold no grudge and would like to meet you. A parley, so to speak, appears in order."*
>
> The Pueblo Chieftain
October 10, 1967

For two days, Harry King had seen no trace of his sister's three-year-old Appaloosa, Lady. That was odd since the horse usually showed up at the ranch house every evening for water and a ration of grain.

There had been a lot of strange goings-on here in the San Luis Valley of southern Colorado in the past few months. Several people had reported seeing unidentifiable flying objects darting about the night sky. One resident had chatted with a tourist who claimed he was from another universe.

King decided he'd better investigate, just to make sure the horse was okay. He'd gone only a quarter of a mile from home before he found the poor animal—dead and mutilated in a bizarre manner that would make headlines nationwide.

King's sister, Nellie Lewis, pastured her horse at her brother's ranch twenty miles northeast of Alamosa in part because of the excellent forage there. Chico, sage, rabbitbrush, and grass flourished in the foothills of the Sangre de Cristo Mountains. It was in a small, flat clearing in the brush that King found Lady on September 9, 1967. The mare was lying on her side. There were no visible wounds on her body, but every scrap of flesh and skin from her head and neck was gone. Her skull and upper vertebrae were so white and clean they looked like they'd bleached in the sun for months. There wasn't a spot of blood or a footprint in sight. Horrified, King rushed home to call his sister and brother-in-law in Alamosa.

The next day, a Sunday, King led the Lewises to the carcass, and the three of them inspected the site more thoroughly. What they found did nothing for their peace of mind. Nellie thought she smelled an odor like incense or something medicinal. Her husband, Berle, could find no hoofprints within one hundred feet of the body.

The Lewises reported their horse's death to the Alamosa County sheriff, who without ever going to look at Lady attributed it to lightning. A game warden agreed. Lightning, or perhaps a bear or mountain lion, must have killed the horse, he concluded without viewing the corpse.

Frustrated at this indifference on the part of the authorities, Mrs. Lewis took her story to *The Pueblo Chieftain*. On October 5, the newspaper proclaimed in a page-one banner headline: "Death of Horse Near Alamosa Creates Mystery." For some reason, the reporter got the name and gender of the horse wrong and called her Snippy, which actually was the name of one of the Lewises other horses. The mistake was never corrected, and the mare remained Snippy in all subsequent media accounts, as well as in the minds of the public. To avoid confusion, she'll continue to be called Snippy here.

Still, the error didn't negate the disagreeable details of the story, and Mrs. Lewis gave the *Chieftain* a graphic description of what she had seen.

> We speculated that Snippy had been struck by lightning, but there were no burns or singe. The meat was pink and fresh and wasn't dried over. Also, there was no blood running out of the carcass, and no blood on the ground nearby....
>
> [The flesh of the head] wasn't hacked off—[the incision] was very neat and that was what was so odd....
>
> We investigated the surrounding area [again] on September 16, and about 100 yards southeast of the horse we found black spots on the ground that looked like those a car exhaust would make. These were about 12 to 18 inches in diameter, and irregular in shape. About 15 of them were found in an area about 100 yards across and 50 yards wide.... A three-foot-tall chico bush had been crushed to within three inches of the ground. For a 10-foot radius around the bush, the sandy ground appeared to have been smoothed out.

In the center of the crushed bush, Mrs. Lewis said, she found a piece of flesh-colored material about the size and shape of a chicken liver.

> There was a small tuft of hair from the mane or tail of the horse sticking to it. With the others standing around, I broke this glob open with a stick. A light green paste oozed out of it. There was no smell. I jerked the hair loose with my left hand, but the hair felt sticky so I dropped it immediately.

Her fingers turned red and began to burn, she said. They continued to sting until she reached the ranch house and washed her hands. Later, at her request, a local man went over the area with a Geiger counter, and Mrs. Lewis told the *Chieftain* he found moderate traces of radiation.

Immediately, people began to speculate about the cause of the mysterious mutilation. Mrs. Lewis's eighty-seven-year-old mother, Agnes King, fueled the discussion further when she claimed she'd seen "a large object" pass over the ranch house on the very night Snippy disappeared. Her eyesight was poor, so she wasn't sure what it was, but it didn't take long before some folks in the San Luis Valley were attributing Snippy's death to sadistic aliens from outer space. Those with a more down-to-earth attitude suspected a gruesome hoax.

From then on, things just got curiouser and curiouser. Sightings of UFOs soared not just in the valley—where, one newspaper suggested, "some residents see unidentified flying objects more often than they see their neighbors"—but throughout the West.

A skeptic with a sense of humor painted a message on an unused billboard just outside of town: "Welcome to Alamosa, Home of Snippy, Flying Saucer Capitol of the World. Beware of Low Flying UFOs. We May Be Looking for You."

In an interview with the Alamosa newspaper, a local artist recalled an eerie conversation she'd had the previous June at an art sale. A man who appeared to be about thirty-five years old and who claimed to be "not from your universe" expressed interest in buying a painting she had done from memory of a UFO she said she'd seen.

"I told him the UFO picture was not for sale, but when I saw he really wanted it, named a high price," she told the Alamosa *Valley Courier*. "He said he had no money with him but would be back some time in October to get the picture." He drove away in a car with Arizona license plates and never returned.

Folks in Alamosa started a memorial fund to finance a monument to Snippy. It seemed appropriate, they thought, to erect a fiberglass statue of the unfortunate beast in the city park. Although they managed to collect $100 on the first day of the fund drive, the monument never materialized.

On October 9, the *Chieftain* reported more alarming news. An autopsy performed on the month-old carcass revealed an empty abdominal cavity. All of the horse's internal organs were missing, although the abdomen showed no signs of having been entered in any way. The autopsy was performed by "a prominent pathologist and blood specialist from Denver who wished to remain anonymous." He also noted that the horse's brain was missing, and there was an inexplicable lack of fluid in the spinal column.

Twenty years later, the pathologist, Dr. John Henry Altshuler, went public with his findings in an interview with Linda Moulton Howe, a journalist producing a documentary about bizarre animal deaths and mutilations. His confession later appeared in her 1989 book *An Alien Harvest*.

> I had heard about all the mysterious lights being seen in the San Luis Valley. The stories provoked my intellectual curiosity. I was just getting started in my profession as a hematologist and did not want anyone to know I was going to investigate the reported UFOs.... I was afraid I would lose my job.

Dr. Altshuler spent a night at Great Sand Dunes National Monument thirty-eight miles northeast of Alamosa. At about two or three in the morning, he saw

> ...three very bright, white lights moving together slowly below the Sangre de Cristo mountain tops. I knew there were no roads up on those rugged mountains, so the lights could not be cars. They were definitely not the illusion of stars moving.... At the time I was both elated and disbelieving in a way. I knew the lights were not my imagination, that the stories about UFOs were true.

The next day, the pathologist examined Snippy's body. What he found frightened him so much he couldn't eat or sleep.

When I got close to the horse, I could see that it was also cut from the neck down to the base of the chest in a vertical, clean incision.

At the edge of the cut, there was a darkened color as if the flesh had been opened and cauterized with a surgical cauterizing blade. The outer edges of the cut skin were firm, almost as if they had been cauterized with a modern day laser. But there was no surgical laser technology like that in 1967....

Most amazing was the lack of blood. I have done hundreds of autopsies. You can't cut into a body without getting some blood. But there was no blood on the skin or on the ground....

Then inside the horse's chest, I remember the lack of organs. Whoever did the cutting took the horse's heart, lungs, and thyroid.

The same day that Dr. Altshuler performed his autopsy, a team of investigators for the National Investigations Committee on Aerial Phenomenon arrived to check out Snippy's death. They reached no immediate conclusions. Instead, one member said, their inquiry simply added to the mystery surrounding the horse's fate.

"Perhaps this may prove to be some new, unknown pestilence," one of them suggested.

The Colorado Society for the Investigation of Unexplained Phenomenon also conducted an on site study and concluded that the incident was no hoax. No one could have smuggled in the equipment needed to strip the head without leaving tracks, the group's report said.

By this time, Coloradans who believed in the apparent invasion of UFOs were practically hysterical. Nonbelievers, on the other hand, found the whole situation amusing. A writer for *The Pueblo Chieftain* let his imagination gallop in an editorial headlined "All Right, Martians, Quit Horsin' Around."

> We mean you no harm, Martians (or whoever you are). But we do wish you would quit this flying-about at night, scaring innocent folks, without ever being decent enough to walk up and say hello.
>
> Please land your saucer in the parking lot at The Pueblo Chieftain, come inside and introduce yourself to any reporter. We'll give you a nice write-up, and even run your picture and a photo of your saucer.

Needless to say, no one took the *Chieftain* up on its offer.

On October 11, Red Fenwick, a writer for *The Denver Post* and self-proclaimed "expert on things Western, including dead horses," put forth his own "simple Western explanation" of Snippy's death in a page-one article.

"Any old-time rancher who's ever slaughtered his own beef out on the range would recognize the evidence in this case without much indulgence in fancy," he insisted.

Fenwick went on to suggest that someone "dropped" Snippy by shooting her with a tranquilizer pellet. Using a "pole rig" with a block and tackle, the pranksters then hauled the animal up by its hind legs and dipped its head into an acid bath.

> The acid would remove the flesh and leave the skeletal head. It likewise would destroy the

animal's brain and other flesh, and it also would account for complete drainage of the horse's body fluids which were reportedly mysteriously absent.

The weight on the base of the poles used in the rig would account for the circle of "strange holes" in the ground.

Splatters of acid around the scene of the operation would explain the "exhaust burns" left by the "flying saucers...."

The presence of acid would explain why Mrs. Berle Lewis' hand "burned and turned red" when she picked up a piece of hide-covered flesh which she found near Snippy's body....

A sprinkling at the site of some finely ground uranium ore, easily obtainable in Colorado, would account for the radiation effect on the geiger counter... and would greatly enhance the element of mystery....

Somewhere an angry sheriff's officer may ferret out a group of young practical jokers laughing their heads off over a cruel hoax that had national repercussions.

But Fenwick wasn't the only one with a theory about Snippy's death, as he soon learned to his chagrin. After his article appeared in the paper, he was deluged with letters—some serious, some not. One woman thought the incident was "just another come-on proposition to boost trade in Alamosa," perpetrated, presumably, by the Alamosa Chamber of Commerce. Others suggested:

• Snippy had been hit by a tornado and the whirling wind had simply stripped the meat from her head.

- Snippy had "lost his head" over some female horse.
- Snippy had fallen and been victimized by a legion of voracious Colorado ants. (The writer had vacationed in the state and said her kids were all but eaten alive by the pests during a family picnic.)
- Snippy was lassooed by Venus Roundup Riders, according to a Mr. U. F. Owe, of Aspen, Colorado.
- Snippy must have drunk some coffee in the same Alamosa cafe in which an anonymous couple had dined. "It sure would have taken out his innards," they wrote.

Fenwick was miffed by the reaction to his column. "It just goes to prove that whatever line you're in, you hadn't better interfere with people's dreams of awful things by presenting some logical explanation," he lamented.

Although plenty of people were having barnloads of fun at Snippy's expense, there were those who took the whole event seriously. A special research team at the University of Colorado, selected by the U.S. Air Force to investigate UFOs, sent three experts to the San Luis Valley hoping to allay fears of a Martian invasion. The nuclear physicist, psychologist, and veterinarian issued this statement:

> There is some evidence that a severe infection had been present in the right flank area. An infection of this nature can kill a horse in a short time.
>
> There is some evidence that the skin in front of the shoulder was incised. This might mean that someone found the horse down

and suffering and cut the throat to stop the suffering.

The skin incision may have given birds and normal predators a chance to clean the neck area of muscle before other parts of the body.

As far as the Kings and Lewises were concerned, this theory was full of holes. It didn't account for the strange odor or lack of footprints. And surely, Mrs. Lewis said, someone finding the horse sick would have walked the quarter-mile to the ranch house to tell its owners.

Another team of scientists from the Desert Research Institute of the University of Nevada analyzed bits of hair, flesh, and "other material" from Snippy, as well as soil samples, and elected to support the "struck-by-lightning" theory.

Throughout September, October, November, and December, people continued to play what the *Rocky Mountain News* called "the now famous game, Pin the Tale on Snippy." Meanwhile, the body of the unfortunate horse lay rotting where it had fallen. Finally, in late December, Dr. Wallace Leary, an Alamosa veterinarian, asked the Lewises if he could have Snippy's remains. He wanted to assemble a horse skeleton to use for anatomical study, and Mrs. Lewis consented. Leary loaded the ripe carcass into a pickup, took it to his clinic, and boiled the flesh from Snippy's bones.

In the course of this grisly business, Leary made a surprising discovery which he shared with *The Denver Post*.

> The hind parts were the last into the pot and it was then discovered for the first time that Snippy had been shot—at least twice. A bullet

hole was found in the left pelvis and one in the right thigh bone. To double check this, X-ray tests were made and lead fragments were found in the holes.

Apparently, no one had bothered to turn Snippy's carcass over to look at the other side.

Leary developed his own theory about Snippy's death. He believed that someone shot the horse as it grazed. The panicked animal ran into a nearby barbed-wire fence, which slashed its neck. Bleeding profusely, it continued running until it fell dead.

Apparently no one will ever know exactly what happened to Snippy the Headless Horse—no one, that is, except the extra-terrestrial or the deviant trickster who may have been responsible. The rest of us may have to settle for a whopping good story, because the answer to this riddle is as elusive as a UFO.

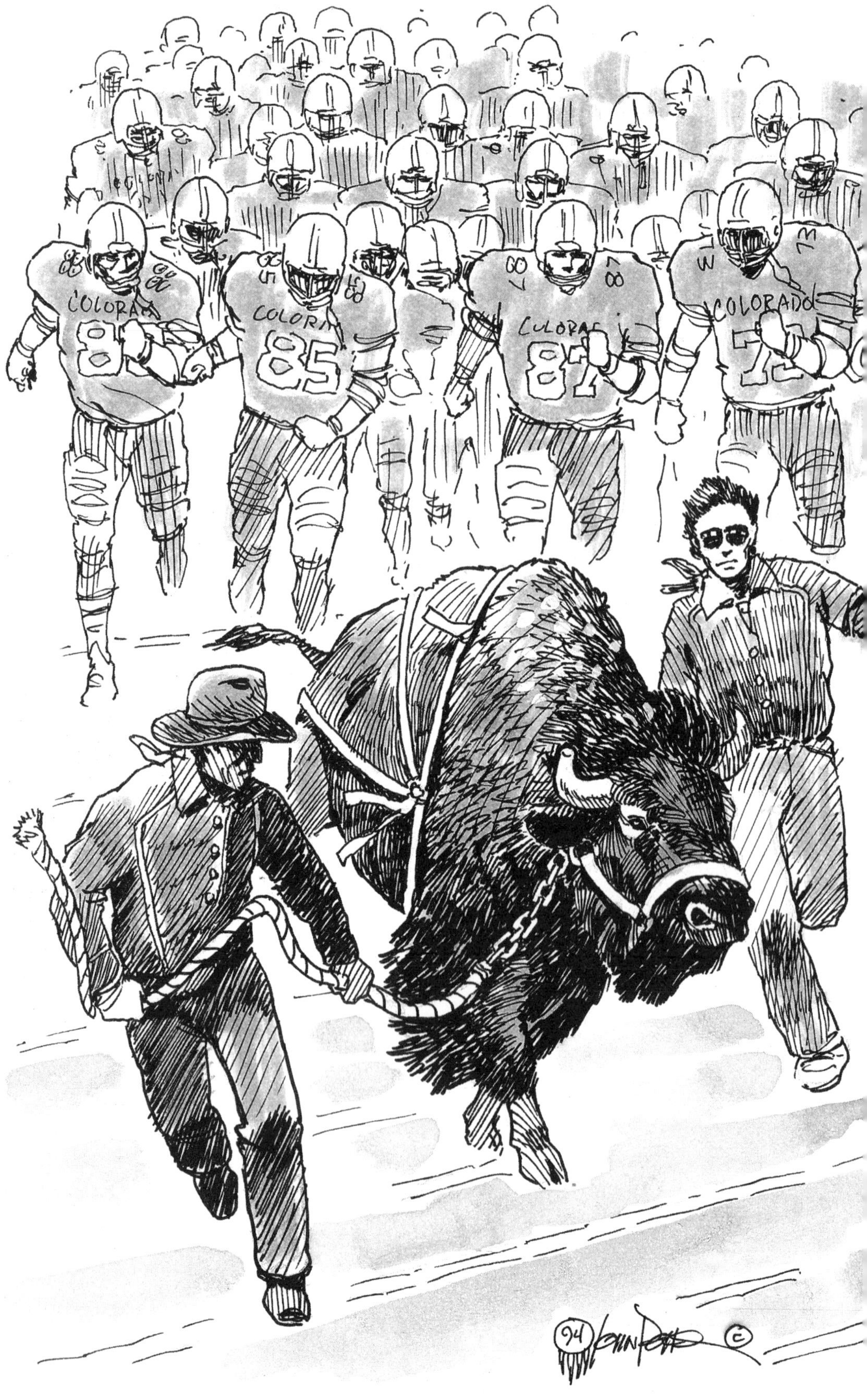
COLORADO
85

Ralphie

BUFFALOES' GAL

> *"The pre-game and second half charges of Ralphie around the perimeter of the playing field (and often through the ranks of startled visiting teams) has been one of the great spectacles of college football."*
>
> Fred Casotti
> *CU Century*

Forty-thousand fans rose to their feet and thundered their welcome as the University of Colorado football team stampeded onto Folsom Field. At the front of this bobbing mass of silver and gold ran the newest member of the team—a mere kid, and a girl at that. But Ralphie, who weighed in at close to three hundred pounds, could easily hold her own against the toughest of linebackers. After all, the rest of the guys were only Buffaloes in spirit. Ralphie was a buffalo in fact.

It was a freshman student from Lubbock, Texas, who decided the CU Buffaloes needed a live mascot to boost team spirit. His father paid a Colorado rancher $150 for the five-month-old bison and donated it to the university in the spring of 1966. Folks initially thought the timid animal was a male, and the student body voted to name it "Ralph" after the bawling sound it made when it ran. When a shrewd student noticed the gender blunder, its name was changed to Ralphie.

For the next thirteen years, Ralphie would attend every home game—and some out-of-town games—played by the CU football team. At the beginning of each half, she would lead the charge as the suited players poured out of the locker room and onto the turf. Her job was to set the opposing team trembling in its cleats at this incarnation of Buffalo brawn.

Ralphie's debut boded well for the Buffs. She presided over a 10-0 shutout of Kansas State on October 1, 1966. CU finished the season with seven wins and three losses.

At the outset of the 1967 season, Ralphie presented her handlers with a new challenge. The previous year she'd been a shy, wide-eyed calf. Now she was a no-nonsense, six-hundred-pound cow. The five students who had escorted her to last year's games took one look and mutinied. They recruited five new wranglers to assume the job of parading her around the stadium.

"The Men in Ralphie's Life," as these wranglers came to be known, used a harness and ropes to control the bison's gridiron gambols. Two men ran alongside her head and two at her sides to steer her, while one rode drag in the rear, doing his best to apply the brakes. All five had to rush full tilt to keep up with their charge, who often reached a speed of twenty-five miles an hour. They vehemently denied rumors that Ralphie was tranquilized before games, but they did confess to taking her for a long run around her pasture on a ranch north of Boulder, just to let off a little steam.

Still, Ralphie was more than a handful. A reporter for the Boulder *Daily Camera* once colorfully described her explosions onto the field.

> What true-blue, dyed-in-the-wool, sit through the rain, sleet, hail and brimstone Buff fan... does not feel his heart thump when he catches that first glimpse of Ralphie charging down the football field, head down, looking a mean no-fool'n wild beast of the West....
>
> During the half time, fire-breathing, earth-shaking Ralphie runs a tour of the field dragging her... handlers behind like they were mere barnacles clinging to the underbelly of a great, surging, cloven-hoof, shaggy whale.

Obviously, not just anyone could become a "Ralphie runner." As one of them once explained, "It takes someone who is gutsy, fast, and has some amount of physical strength." Only seasoned athletes—particularly those with football and/or track experience—were eligible for the job. Like other university athletes, they were awarded a varsity letter for their Herculean efforts.

Ralphie quickly became popular with CU students, and in 1968 she ran for student-body president. Her campaign slogan, stapled to copies of the $34,000 student budget, was "What's It to You?" Her foray into politics was unsuccessful, but that was probably for the best. Her responsibilities as mascot already took a hefty bite out of her grazing and cud-chewing time.

The campus got further proof of Ralphie's popularity in 1971, when she was elected homecoming queen. She was crowned during half-time at the homecoming game against Missouri, but she showed her disdain for such foolishness by dumping the crown onto the Astroturf.

A mascot as impressive and conspicuous as Ralphie made a tempting target for pranksters loyal to opposing teams. And sure enough, in 1970 she became the victim of a kidnapping attempt. The *Daily Camera* huffily reported the incident.

> It takes a real low down, no good, sneaky sidewinder—and also a nut—to steal a pregnant buffalo, and six cadets from the Air Force Academy pleaded guilty to every count this morning in confessing they rustled CU's rotund Ralphie overnight.
>
> Furthermore, the six, from the Academy's 21st Squadron, said they would not bring the babied beast out of hiding at Colorado Springs until 1 p.m. today when the Air Force and Colorado football teams meet on the field of battle.
>
> Then she was to be paraded around Falcon Stadium as a base buffalo burger... with two make-believe buns strapped to her sides and cadets holding a six-foot catsup bottle over her.

The cadets admitted they had tried to steal Ralphie a week earlier, but they had to abort the mission when they found the bison, reportedly pregnant, wouldn't fit into the trailer they had brought. This time, they said, they borrowed a truck and a six-horse trailer for the job and coaxed the bulky mascot inside with alfalfa sticks.

"There was a rumor we got the wrong buffalo and a male besides," one of the cadets said. "So we called a vet. Its Ralphie, all right. Not only is she a she, but she eats about a ton of hay an hour."

After pulling off the heist, the cadets returned Ralphie unharmed, but the indignant Buffs got their revenge. They pounded the Air Force 49-19.

The rumors of Ralphie's delicate condition turned out to be true, but tragically, she gave birth to her first calf during a mid-October snowstorm. The poor thing froze to death before anyone knew of its existence. It wasn't until the spring of 1972, when a second calf was born, that Ralphie could celebrate her first Mother's Day. Students voted to name her daughter Buffy. The father was a fifteen-year-old, 1,800-pound bull named Barney, known best for his ugly face, short temper, and long horns.

But fate was cruel to Ralphie, for the next fall Buffy died of pneumonia. A year and a half later, the CU mascot gave birth to yet another female calf. This one was named Streaker because she liked to streak through the pasture in pursuit of butterflies, her mother, and her father, Barney. This one also died young, of a brain concussion.

Finally, in 1975, Ralphie gave birth to a healthy calf named Spirit because she was "so full of steam" and play. The little heifer made her first public appearance at the 1975 homecoming game, surprising spectators who hadn't known Ralphie was a mother yet again.

"We had bad luck with Ralphie's... other babies so we didn't want to make a splash of this one," the bison's handler told the local newspaper.

In 1978, word went out that Ralphie, now twelve years old, was going to retire. Her trainer said she was getting too old and her bones too brittle to be galloping around a football field. So she made her last official appearance at the CU-Iowa State game on November 18 and was honored at a special ceremony, including champagne, at half-time. A new bison mascot, Ralphie II, made her debut at the same game.

The tradition that began with Ralphie continues to be a colorful part of CU football. When Ralphie II died of a heart attack in 1987, Ralphie III took the field, and a Ralphie IV waits in the wings to replace her when she retires.

The original Ralphie died of natural causes in May 1982 after spending her retirement grazing and dozing in her pasture at Hidden Valley Ranch. The *Daily Camera* paid her tribute with an obituary on its editorial page.

> It was with nostalgia and a surge of the old yelling-in-the-stands pride that we noted the death last Thursday of Ralphie, the Golden Buffalo who set the standard for all yet to come.
>
> Ralphie was just a child when she became the University of Colorado's mascot. But if anyone thought she was there to be cute, she soon made it clear that such was not her idea of the role.
>
> She roared and she charged, showing little mercy for her cage or her handlers during pre-game exhibitions in the football stadium....
>
> What could compare, after all, with this real, live, charging buffalo...? What kind of inspiration can a team get from nicknames like Sooners, Cowboys, or Cornhuskers—characters who seem more friendly than ferocious? And

what are the chances of a Big 8 school organizing a cyclone on the field at the right time?

Only in Ralphie were all the attributes of an ideal mascot to be found.... We assume that her successor, a youngster named Ralphie II, has found that the original is always a tough act to follow.

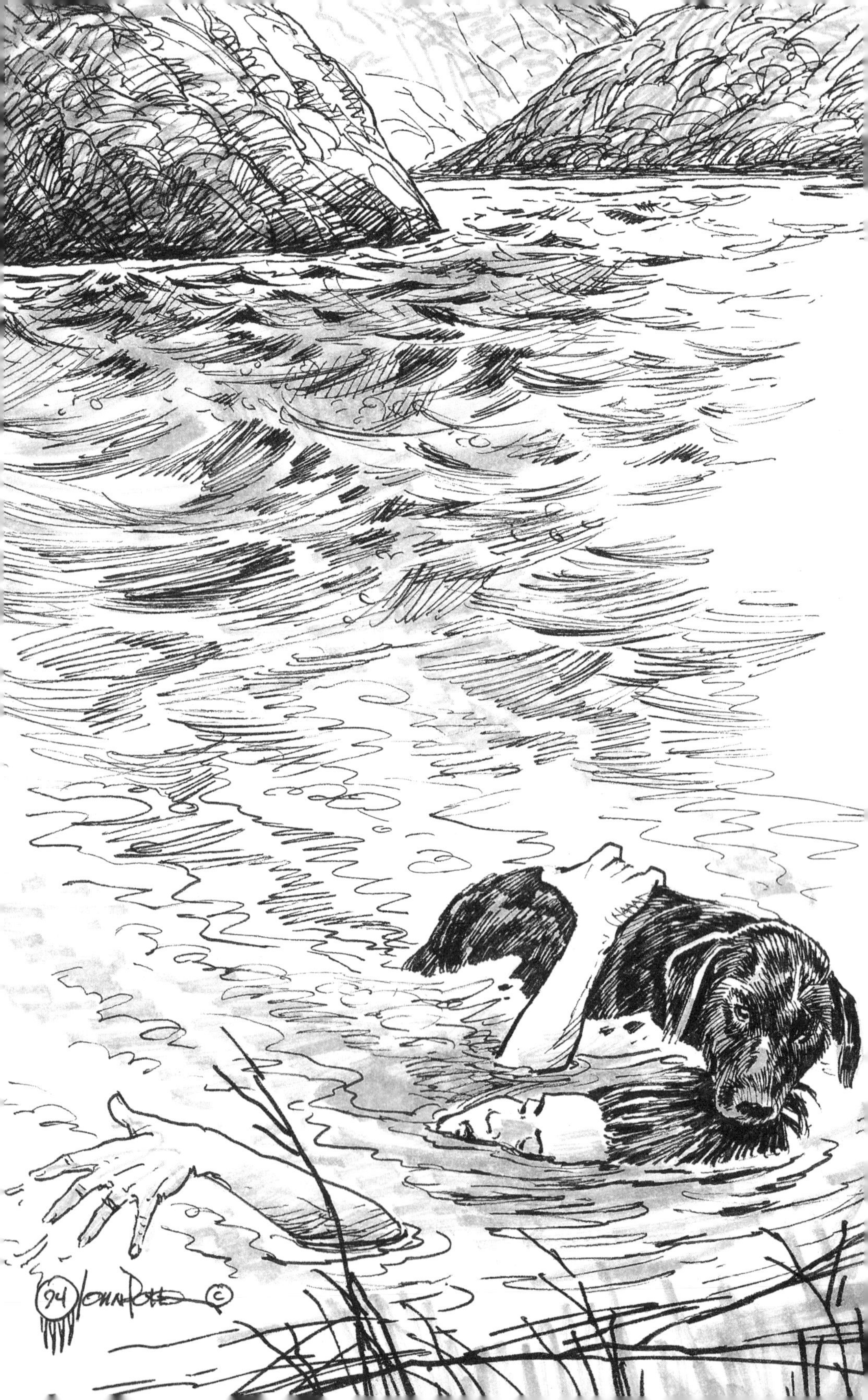

Bo
WHITEWATER HERO

> *"When the Man waked up he said, 'What is Wild Dog doing here?' And the Woman said, 'His name is not Wild Dog any more, but the First Friend, because he will be our friend for always and always and always.'"*
>
> Rudyard Kipling
> *Just So Stories*

A foaming wave leaped over the bow of the raft, drenching its occupants, Rob and Laurie Roberts and their dogs, Bo and Dutchess. Laurie sucked in her breath as the icy water soaked through her shirt. Her heart pounded like whitewater rapids. This Sunday morning excursion down the Colorado River was definitely exhilarating a bit too exhilarating, perhaps.

It was early June 1982 when the Robertses rounded a bend in the river east of Glenwood Springs and slid into Maintenance Rapid. Now the raft bucked and spun, oblivious to their attempts to steer it. It plunged into a trough between waves and reared up to climb the other side. The six-foot wall of water flipped it like a pancake.

Before they realized what was happening, the Robertses and their pets tumbled into the raging river.

Rob surfaced downstream and looked around him for Laurie. He watched as Bo bobbed out from under the raft, but his wife was still nowhere to be seen. Horrified, he realized she must be trapped beneath it. He struggled against the swift current, trying to go to her rescue. Precious minutes passed.

Meanwhile, Laurie somersaulted under the water, disoriented and frantic. She couldn't find the surface. Her lungs were bursting. She gulped water and smashed against the rocks on the river bottom. Then something gripped her hair and began pulling her through the water.

As Rob floundered helplessly downstream, he saw Bo dive back under the raft. When the Labrador next appeared, he had Laurie's hair clamped in his teeth, and he pulled her clear of the sinking boat. Once she was free of it, she grabbed Bo's tail and let him tow her to shore.

That night, nine-month-old Bo dined on steak, compliments of his grateful owners. Three-month-old Duchess was found safe the next day.

To the Robertses, Bo was nothing short of a hero, another Lassie or Rin Tin Tin. "I felt I was going to drown," Laurie later said. "If it weren't for Bo I know I wouldn't be alive today."

Bo's brave deed impressed not only his owners but the people at the Quaker Oats Company, makers of Ken-L Ration dog food. Since 1954, the company had been honoring the courage and devotion of canine heroes across the nation. In 1982, it named Bo its Dog Hero of the Year. With his owners, the bemused pup flew to Boston in October to attend a banquet in his honor. He was presented with a $1,000 savings bond, a gold-plated leash and collar, and—best of all to Bo's way of thinking—a year's supply of dog food.

On October 22, the mayor of Glenwood Springs proclaimed "Bo Day" in honor of the hometown hero. The chocolate Lab posed for the newspaper photographer and shook paws with the mayor. Bo was probably bewildered by all the fuss the two-legged types were making. As he patiently endured their fawning and petting, he may well have wished folks would just let him get home to all that tasty dog food.

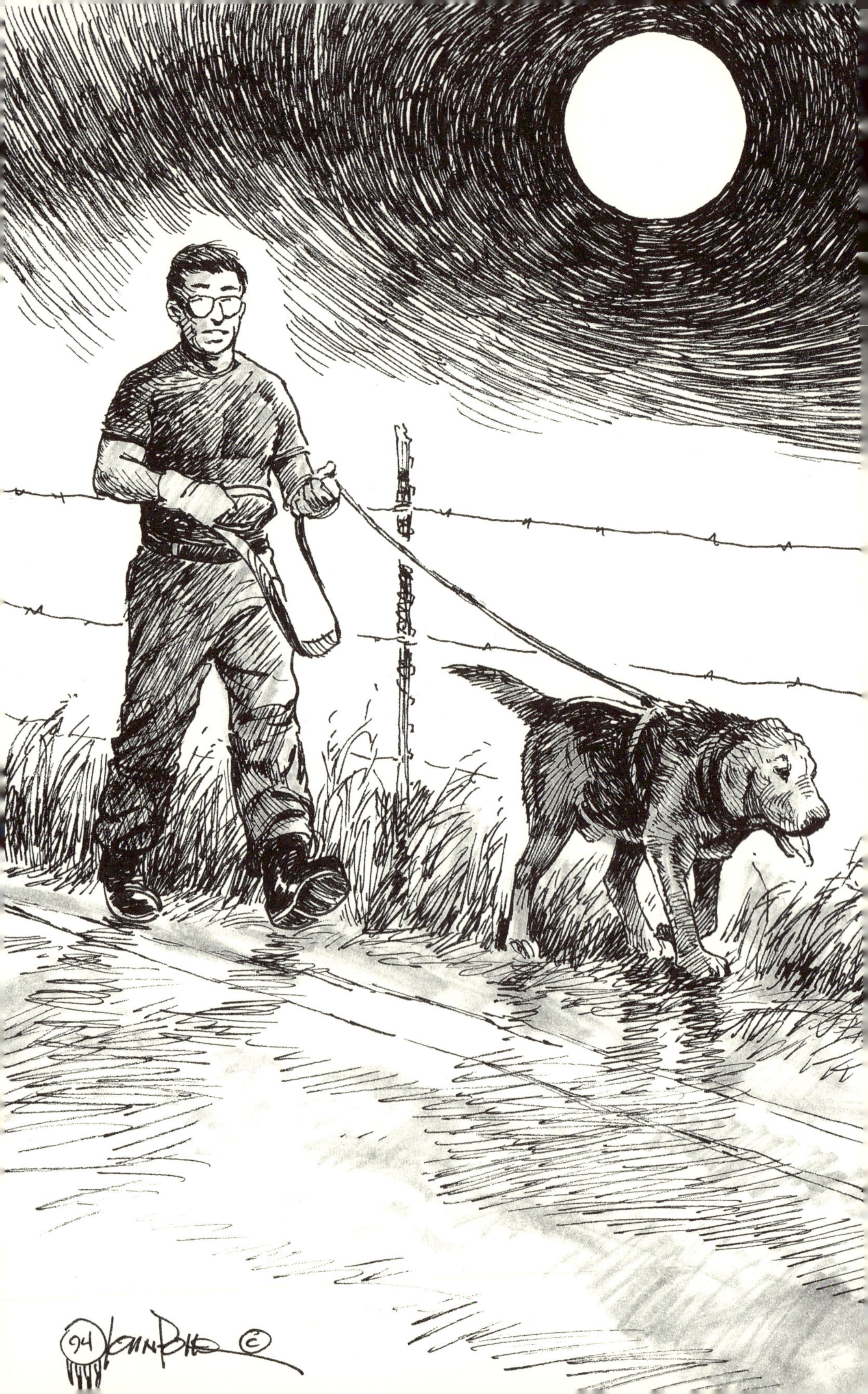

YOGI

SUPER SLEUTH

"Yogi the bloodhound is Colorado's miracle dog."

Headline, *The Denver Post*
May 26, 1993

Alie Berrelez was one of those kids who can't help but make people smile. A spunky five-year-old, she had dimples when she laughed and soft doelike eyes that sparkled below a ragged fringe of coffee-colored hair. She loved to fly kites, to dance to Little Richard songs, and to watch *The Little Mermaid* on TV. She giggled her way into the hearts of her neighbors and had just shared a pizza with one of them when Alie Berrelez disappeared.

Alie's neighbor was one of the last people to see the child alive on that tragic evening in May 1993. She left the little girl sitting outside her Englewood apartment while she slipped back inside to put away the leftovers. When she returned moments later, Alie was gone.

"She knew better [than to go with strangers]," Alie's distraught mother told a reporter the next day. "But she's also only five years old. She loved people, and that was one of the things that made her special. Now I'm afraid it was one of the things that made her a victim."

Police launched a door-to-door search of the Denver suburb, while friends and family kept a hopeful vigil at the Berrelez home. Newspaper headlines begged Alie's kidnapper to release her so she could get the asthma medicine she needed to help her breathe. Local businessmen began raising reward money for information leading to her safe return.

Despite the concerted effort, police were stymied. Three days after Alie's disappearance, they had no clues, no suspects, and "a lot of frustration." So they decided to call in a specialist: a canine "cop" known as Yogi.

A bloodhound with floppy ears and enough skin to cover two dogs, Yogi is a member of the K-9 Unit of the Aurora (Colorado) Police Department, and he's blessed, according to his handler, Officer Jerry Nichols, with "an incredible nose" for tracking. Since joining the force in 1991, he's worked on more than three hundred cases in three states, including forty homicides. He's helped put seven murderers behind bars.

Still, the Berrelez case seemed like too much to ask, even of talented Yogi. Days had passed since Alie's disappearance, rain had fallen, and hundreds of people had tramped through the neighborhood in their search for the missing girl. The kidnapper had probably abducted Alie by car and was most likely miles away by now. Englewood police doubted that Yogi could pick up the trail.

But skeptics didn't faze Yogi. Starting from the front step of the apartment building where the Berrelez family lived, the dog beat a steady path, following the scent he'd picked up from a piece of Alie's clothing. Tail up and nose down, straining against the long leash held by Nichols, he trotted confidently toward Broadway, one of the busiest thoroughfares in the Denver area. He snuffled down Broadway for several blocks and led officers onto the interstate. The searchers hopped into a patrol car and headed west on Colorado 470 past Chatfield Reservoir, stopping to let Yogi out at each exit until he found the point at which the kidnapper had left the highway.

After about seven hours and ten miles of tracking, Yogi was wilting in a midday sun so hot it could almost melt asphalt. Nichols knew that his dog would keep going until it dropped from exhaustion, so he decided to call it quits for the day.

Englewood police resumed the search the next morning, beginning at the mouth of Deer Creek Canyon, where Yogi had left off. Searchers began combing the woods along the two-lane blacktop road that climbed through the canyon and into the foothills of the Rockies. Just before noon, two of them found a khaki duffel bag at the bottom of a twenty-foot embankment, only a couple of feet from Deer Creek and only a mile or so from where Yogi had stopped the day before.

The hunt for Alie Berrelez was over. The girl's body was stuffed inside, still dressed in the OshKosh denim jumper she'd been wearing when she disappeared. Precious Alie had smothered to death.

Though the Berrelez story has no happy ending, Yogi did at least free Alie's relatives from the limbo they'd endured for five long days.

"In a way, we haven't lost her because she's with the Lord," Alie's grandfather said in a stoic statement to

The Denver Post. "We feel better knowing that we don't have to worry anymore."

Yogi had yet another contribution to make to the Berrelez case. The day after Alie's body was found, he and Nichols returned to Deer Creek Canyon to try to pick up the scent of the girl's killer and trace it back to its source. The trail led back to a neighboring apartment in the Englewood complex where Alie had lived, leading police to believe that a neighbor committed the crime. By June 1994, officers still hadn't made an arrest but were working to gather enough evidence to make a case against their prime suspect. If the case goes to trial, Yogi may well become an important "witness." Bloodhounds are the only dogs whose work can be considered as evidence in court.

Yogi's role in the Berrelez case attracted the attention and admiration of people far beyond Denver and its sprawling suburbs. The National Police Hall of Fame awarded the dog a medal for "outstanding canine service," and the Colorado Legislature presented him with a commendation for meritorious service. The impressed lawmakers invited the hound right onto the floor of the House to get both his award and some appreciative pats on the head.

"They don't give those [awards] to dogs very often," Nichols proudly pointed out. But as the officer himself once said, "[Yogi] did all the work. All I did was hang on for the ride."

In 1994, ABC featured Yogi in its weekly news magazine program, *Day One*, comparing him with the fictional bloodhound who died stalking Paul Newman in *Cool Hand Luke*.

In 1993—four days after Alie's body was found—the *Post* called Yogi a "miracle dog" and howled his praises.

Even the experts were dumbfounded by the abilities of Yogi, a common-looking bloodhound with extraordinarily uncommon skills....

"This is probably one of the longer tracks by a police dog," search coordinator Sgt. Byron Wicks said of Yogi's work last week. "I have never heard of such a thing."

Following the scent for 10 miles, along busy traffic thoroughfares, was an impressive accomplishment. But following the scent after three nights and two days had passed was even more impressive.

Experts explain that human dander carries a person's unique scent and acts much like an airborne pollen, dispersed onto the ground and vegetation along its path. The explanation is, at the same time, both sensible and also unbelievable.

But to most civilian observers, Yogi's performance was nothing short of miraculous.

According to Nichols, Yogi can stalk a person traveling in a car even if the windows are rolled up, because the person's scent can seep out of the vehicle and onto the pavement, sidewalk, curbs, and vegetation nearby. It can remain there for as long as a month. Rain actually enhances the scent and makes the hound's job easier.

Yogi began his career in law enforcement not long after Nichols bought him for $350 from a Colorado Springs bloodhound breeder in 1989. The officer was planning to name his pet Fred, but his wife and oldest son vetoed the idea and christened him Yogi instead.

For about a year, Nichols tutored Yogi with the help of a Jefferson County sheriff's deputy who had trained two hounds for his own agency. In the fall of 1990, Nichols started using Yogi in missing-person cases, and by August of 1991, he'd convinced his superiors that the goofy-looking bloodhound would make a valuable addition to the force. Now the pooch doggedly patrols the streets each night from the back of his master's police truck.

Nichols doesn't try to hide the fact that he has mixed feelings about his tongue-lolling, tail-thumping partner. On the one hand, Nichols acknowledges, the bloodhound "will out-track and out-run any other dog."

"The bloodhound is very unique," he said. "There's no dog that will work harder for you. They'll run themselves to death."

"These dogs have an innate sense of smell that has no equal...," he once told the *Post*. "Tracking is their life."

On the other hand, Nichols griped, Yogi's a "slob," a "klutz" and a "pain in the butt." The officer wasn't a bit surprised that, in a recent study of canine intelligence, rating more than 140 breeds, the bloodhound finished almost dead last. Nichols often refers to his four-year-old, one-hundred-pound partner as "Bonehead" or "Knucklehead"—but not without a hint of affection in his voice.

The list of Yogi's bad habits is almost as long as the expression on his face. The dog sometimes lets loose with some "very loud and very obnoxious" howls. He drools constantly and likes to chew on anything made of wood—including the siding on Nichols's house.

"He's very affectionate," the officer admitted. "People like him and he likes people. He's very gentle—if you don't mind getting slobbered on. I usually carry a little rag with me."

In fact, at the end of a long day with his nose to the grindstone "his reward is getting to slobber [on] the person he's tracking," Nichols once said.

Fortunately, Yogi's list of accomplishments is even longer than that of his foibles. In addition to the Berrelez girl, he's hunted down a teenager wanted for the murder of a state patrol officer. He helped find three robbers who stole $80,000 from an armored car. He's looked for Alzheimer's patients who've wandered away from home and prisoners who've escaped from jail, drunk drivers who've walked away from accidents and people trapped in collapsed buildings. He's even helped a local historical society locate graves more than one hundred years old.

Alie Berrelez's grandparents were so impressed with Yogi's capabilities that they started a fund to buy bloodhounds for law-enforcement agencies.

"This is a way for them to cope with the loss of Alie," Nichols explained.

By June 1994, they'd placed about a dozen dogs. The first now works for the Cherry Hills (Colorado) Police Department. The Berrelez family named it Alie— in memory of a beloved child who was brutally robbed of her future.

BIBLIOGRAPHY

TALL BULL: BATTLE TROPHY

Cody, William F. *Life and Adventures of Buffalo Bill.* Chicago: John R. Stanton Co., 1917.

Cody, William F. *The Life of Hon. William F. Cody.* Lincoln: University of Nebraska Press, 1978. Originally published in 1879.

Dillon, Richard H. *North American Indian Wars.* New York: Facts on File, 1983.

Grinnell, George Bird. *The Fighting Cheyennes.* Norman: University of Oklahoma Press, 1956. Originally published by Charles Scribner's Sons, 1915.

Price, George F. *Across the Continent with the Fifth Cavalry.* New York: Antiquarian Press, 1959. Originally published in 1883.

Reckmeyer, Clarence. "The Battle of Summit Springs," *The Colorado Magazine*, Nov. 1929.

Russell, Don. *The Lives and Legends of Buffalo Bill.* Norman: University of Oklahoma Press, 1960.

Sell, Henry Blackman, and Victor Weybright. *Buffalo Bill and the Wild West.* New York: Oxford University Press, 1955.

Spring, Agnes Wright. "Buffalo Bill and His Horses," a reprint in pamphlet form of an article in *Livestock Annual of Western Farm Life*, Denver, 1948.

Utley, Robert M., and Wilcomb E. Washburn. *The American Heritage History of the Indian Wars.* New York: American Heritage Publishing Co., 1977.

Wetmore, Helen Cody. *Last of the Great Scouts: Life Story of Col. W.F. Cody (Buffalo Bill).* Duluth, Minn.: Duluth Press Printing Co., 1899.

OLD MOSE: MAN KILLER

Bell, Jack. "King of the Grizzlies is Dead," *The Denver Post*, May 17, 1904.

"Biggest Grizzly in Colorado Is Killed," *The Denver Times*, May 3, 1904.

Epperson, Harry A. *Colorado As I Saw It.* Kaysville, Utah: Inland Printing Co., 1943.

Everett, George G. and Dr. Wendell F. Hutchinson. *Under the Angel of Shavano.* Denver: Golden Bell Press, 1963.

Lancaster, Dr. E.G. "What Old Mose's Brain Shows," *The Denver Post*, May 17, 1904.

"Old Mose Has Bit the Dust," *The Denver Post*, May 3, 1904.

Pigg, Wharton ("Whort"). "Old Mose's Demise," *Outdoor Life*, Vol. 14, 1904.

Queal, Cal. "The Grizzly that Terrorized Colorado," *Empire Magazine*, Jan. 28, 1968.

Sterling, Janet. "A True Bear Story," *The Denver Post*, July 7, 1946. A revised version of this article also appears in *Notorious Grizzly Bears*, by W.P. Hubbard with Seale Harris. Chicago: The Swallow Press, 1960.

Williams, Lester L. "Old Mose, the Great Grizzly," *The Denver Westerners' Roundup*, Jan.-Feb. 1979.

BUFF AND BLAZE: FATAL FOES

Hubbard, W.P., with Seale Harris. *Notorious Grizzly Bears*. Chicago: The Swallow Press, 1960.

PRUNES: PROSPECTOR'S PARTNER

Bair, Everett. "Jack of All Trails," *The Denver Post*, Oct. 16, 1949.

Bancroft, Caroline. *Two Burros of Fairplay*. Boulder, Colo.: Johnson Publishing Co., 1968.

Ellis, Amanda M. *Legends and Tales of the Rockies*. Publisher unnamed, 1954.

Friggens, Myriam. *Tales, Trails and Tommy Knockers: Stories from Colorado's Past*. Boulder, Colo.: Johnson Publishing Co., 1979.

Galbraith, Den. "The Hoax of Prunes the Burro," *The Golden Transcript*, Golden, Colo., Dec. 1, 1969.

Hayes, Albert E. "Prospector Rupe Sherwood Is Going Back to the Hills—Alone," *The Denver Post*, May 17, 1931.

Lindberg, Gene. "Burro Is Slated for Death at Age of 62 Years," *The Denver Post*, April 4, 1930.

"Rupe Sherwood's Ashes Buried Near Grave of Burro," *The Denver Post*, Aug. 31, 1931.

Stout, Joanna. Fairplay historian. Telephone interview with author, April 29, 1994.

Taylor, Ralph C. "Four-Legged 'Founders' of the Frontier," *The Pueblo Chieftain*, Pueblo, Colo., April 9, 1978.

BUM AND SHORTY: INSEPARABLE PALS

Bancroft, Caroline. *Two Burros of Fairplay*. Boulder, Colo.: Johnson Publishing Co., 1968.

Kellogg, Virgil L. "The Strange Friendship of Shorty and Bum," *Empire Magazine*, Sept. 8, 1963.

"A Memorial to Canine Devotion," *Rocky Mountain News*, Denver, May 4, 1959.

SKIPPER: WAR VETERAN

Behan, John M. *Dogs of War*. New York: Charles Scribner's Sons, 1946.

Dempewolff, Richard. *Animal Reveille*. New York: Doubleday, Doran & Co., 1943.

Downey, Fairfax. *Dogs for Defense*. New York: Trustees of Dogs for Defense, Inc., 1955.

———., ed. *Great Dog Stories of All Time*. New York: Doubleday & Co., 1962.

Going, Clayton G. *Dogs at War*. New York: The Macmillan Co., 1945.

Wallace, Robert. *World War II: The Italian Campaign*. Alexandria, Va.: Time-Life Books, 1981.

"War Veteran Skipper Enjoys Peaceful Life," *The Denver Post*, May 15, 1951.

Wels, Byron G. *Animal Heroes*. New York: Macmillan Publishing Co., 1979.

Yoseloff, Thomas [Thomas Young, pseud.]. *Dogs for Democracy*. New York: Bernard Ackerman, Inc., 1944.

Young, Brig. Peter. *Illustrated World War II Encyclopedia*, Vol. 9. Westport, Conn.: H.S. Stuttman Inc., 1966, 1978.

HAMBONE: JUMPIN' FOOL

Dempewolff, Richard. *Animal Reveille*. New York: Doubleday, Doran & Co., 1943.

Fort Carson: A Tradition of Victory. A publication of the Fort Carson, Colo., Public Affairs Office.

"Hambone Dies at Carson," *The Sun*, Colorado Springs, Colo., March 30, 1971.

"Hambone Has Gone on to Happy Grazing Grounds," *Gazette Telegraph*, Colorado Springs, Colo., March 29, 1971.

"Hambone Readied for Annual Pikes Peak Rodeo," *The Denver Post*, July 18, 1962.

"Hambone: The Mule and His Song," *The Sun*, Colorado Springs, Colo., April 24, 1971.

"Hamilton T. Bone Was a Classy Mule at Carson," *Gazette Telegraph*, Colorado Springs, Colo., July 2, 1972.

Marranzino, Pasquale. "A Memorial for Hambone," *Rocky Mountain News*, Denver, March 31, 1971.

"Mule Beats Horses," *Life*, July 4, 1949.

"Post Radio Station Honors Hamilton Bone," *Gazette Telegraph*, Colorado Springs, Colo., April 1, 1973.

Smith, Columbus. "Former Army 'Muleskinners' Recall Good Old Days," *The Sun*, Colorado Springs, Colo., April 17, 1971.

"30-Year-Old Vet Now in Retirement," *The Denver Post*, July 9, 1962.

Wels, Byron G. *Animal Heroes*. New York: Macmillan Publishing Co., 1979.

SHEP: TURNPIKE MASCOT

Bates, Betsy. "Mascot 'Shep': Fond Memories," *The Daily Camera*, Boulder, Colo., April ?, 1980.

Buchanan, John. "Shep's Rest is Undisturbed," *Empire Magazine*, Jan. 9, 1972.

Diddlebock, Bob. "Site Honors Toll-Road Dog That Collected Love," *Rocky Mountain News*, Denver, Nov. 22, 1981.

Gonzales, Darlene. "Shep, the 'Turnpike Mascot,' Lovingly Recalled by SDH," *The Citizen*, a publication of the Colo. Assoc. of Public Employees, Denver, Oct. 1989.

Hall, James. "Partly Shepherd, Mostly Affection," *Boulder Lifestyle Magazine*, Summer 1986.

Harkins, R. Roger. "The Story of Shep, the Dog Who Made the Turnpike His Home," *The Daily Camera*, Boulder, Colo., Sept. 10, 1967.

Lawhon, Morgan. "Turnpike Tollhouse Pet Dead," *The Denver Post*, Aug. 4, 1964.

Severson, Thor. "Rites Mark Pike Opening," *The Denver Post*, Jan. 20, 1952.

"$6 Million Turnpike Opens Officially," *The Denver Post*, Jan. 20, 1952.

"State to Dedicate New Turnpike Today," *The Denver Post*, Jan. 19, 1952.

"Thousands Expected to Crowd Pike Today," *The Denver Post*, Jan. 20, 1952.

ELIJAH: HARRIED HERMIT

The Denver Post, almost daily articles April 5-25 and May 21-29, 1956.

"Dude Ranchers Honor Elijah at Hall of Fame," *Gazette Telegraph*, Colorado Springs, Colo., Jan. 3, 1975.

Fenwick, Red. "Elijah's Finished His Last Winter," *The Denver Post*, Sept. 9, 1971.

"Haylift to the Peak," *Newsweek*, April 23, 1956.

"High-Flying Haylift for a Hard-Luck Horse," *Life*, April 30, 1956.

"'Horse on Mountain' Preserved in Stone," *The Denver Post*, Dec. 13, 1974.

Hosokawa, Bill. "Elijah, the Hermit Horse," *The Reader's Digest*, Sept. 1956. The article is reprinted in *Animals You Will Never Forget*, published by The Reader's Digest Assoc., 1969.

Hunt, Corinne. Historian, Brown Palace Hotel, Denver. Telephone interview with author, June 1, 1994.

Letters to the Editor, *The Denver Post*, April 14, 15, 18, 25, 1956.

McWilliams, George. "Tale of 'Elijah,' Snowbound Horse, Circles Globe in Dozen Languages," *The Denver Post*, Feb. 7, 1957.

SNIPPY: HEADLESS HOAX?

(Many of the news stories used in researching this chapter were taken from a file at the Adams State College Library, Alamosa, Colo. In some cases, names of newspapers and dates of publication were not provided.)

"All Right, Martians, Quit Horsin' Around," *The Pueblo Chieftain*, Pueblo, Colo., Oct. 10, 1967.

Brandon, Jim. *Weird America*. New York: E.P. Dutton, 1978.

Dangel, Ray. "Snippy Death Inquiry Shifts into Low Gear," *The Pueblo Chieftain*, Pueblo, Colo., Oct. 10, 1967.

———. "Weird Things Still Zip Through Skies Over SLV," *The Pueblo Chieftain*, Pueblo, Colo., Oct. 6, 1968.

Darling, R. Spencer. "Autopsy Reveals All Organs Missing from Abdomen," *The Pueblo Chieftain*, Pueblo, Colo., Oct. 9, 1967.

———. "Bizarre Death Put Under UFO Probe," *The Pueblo Chieftain*, Pueblo, Colo., Oct. 6, 1967.

"Death of Horse Near Alamosa Creates Mystery," *The Pueblo Chieftain*, Pueblo, Colo., Oct. 5, 1967.

Dunning, John. "Opinion Split on Mystery: UFO or Not—'Who Knows?'" *The Denver Post*, Oct. 12, 1967.

Fenwick, Robert W. ("Red"). "Letters on Horse Make Him Snippy," *The Denver Post*, Oct. 15, 1967.

———. "Old Red Puts Head to Horse Mystery," *The Denver Post*, Oct. 11, 1967.

———. "Snippy Not Alone Without His Spine," *The Denver Post*, Oct. 15, 1967.

"Hoax Possibility Advanced in Death of Alamosa Horse," *The Pueblo Chieftain*, Pueblo, Colo., Oct. 13, 1967.

Howe, Linda Moulton. *An Alien Harvest*. Littleton, Colo.: Linda Moulton Howe Productions, 1989.

Jessen, Kenneth. *Eccentric Colorado*. Boulder, Colo.: Pruett Publishing Co., 1985.

Lewis, Berle. Telephone interview with author, June 11, 1994.

Nicholas, Pearl M. "'I'm Not from Your Universe,'" *Valley Courier*, Alamosa, Colo., Oct. 6, 1967.

———. "Snippy Story Continues in U.S., Foreign Magazines," *Valley Courier*, Alamosa, Colo., no date given.

"Saucer Role Pondered in Ten Deaths," *The Denver Post*, Oct. 10, 1967.

Scher, Zeke. "The Return of Snippy," *Empire Magazine*, Jan. 19, 1969.

"Scientists Blame Lightning in Snippy Death," newspaper unknown, Feb. 11, 1968.

"Several Alamosans Keep Watch on UFOs Since Snippy Death," *The Pueblo Chieftain*, Pueblo, Colo., March 27, 1968.

"Snippy Report in Thai Paper," *The Pueblo Chieftain*, Pueblo, Colo., Feb. 27, 1968.

"Snippy Still on the Move in Alamosa," *The Pueblo Chieftain*, Pueblo, Colo., no date given.

"Snippy's Remains Await UFO Check," *The Denver Post*, Oct. 6, 1967.

Thomas, Bob. "UFO Prober Recounts Snippy Death," *The Pueblo Chieftain*, Pueblo, Colo., Feb. 21, 1971.

"UFO Mystery Intensified by New Reports," *The Denver Post*, Oct. 8, 1967.

"Vet Finds Holes in Snippy Mystery," *Rocky Mountain News*, Denver, Jan. 26, 1968.

RALPHIE: BUFFALOES' GAL

Casotti, Fred. *CU Century: 100 Years of Colorado University Football.* Denver: Original Publications, 1990.

Parker, John. Bison handler and trainer, Boulder, Colo. Telephone interview with author, Sept. 13, 1993.

The following articles were taken from the *Daily Camera*, Boulder, Colo.:

"CU Mascot Ralphie No. 1 Dies in Field," May 14, 1982.

Deans, Sue. "Buffs to Sideline Ralphie Following Today's Game," Nov. 18, 1978.

———. "Ralphie Not Headed for Pasture This Year," Sept. 9, 1978.

"550-Pound Cow Buffalo Has CU Football Spirit," Oct. 10, 1968.

Foehr, Stephen. "CU's Ralphie May Be Big with Buffalo," Sept. 12, 1971.

"New Mascot," photo and caption, March 20, 1966.

"Ralphie Becomes a Mom," April 18, 1974.

"Ralphie Buffaloed; Stolen by Cadets," Nov. 21, 1970.

"Ralphie Enters Student Body Election at CU," Feb. 27, 1968.

"Ralphie Gives Birth to Spirit," Dec. ?, 1975.

"Ralphie Understood Her Role," May 17, 1982.

"Rraalph—CU's Gridiron Coed," Nov. 5, 1967.

Watkins, Robin. "CU's Ralphie to Retire," Nov. 19, 1977.

Wilson, Marc. "Ralphie Shows the Spirit of Motherhood," May 14, 1972.

BO: WHITEWATER HERO

"Dog Day in Glenwood," *Glenwood Post*, Glenwood, Colo., Oct. 22, 1982.

Paludan, Michael. "Bo Must Be a Fan of Lassie," *Glenwood Post*, Glenwood, Colo., June 8, 1982.

Vicha, Jessie. Public Relations specialist, McDowell & Piasecki Food Communications, Chicago. Correspondence with author, Sept. 23, 1993.

YOGI: SUPER SLEUTH

"Day One," a weekly news-magazine program broadcast on ABC, June 13, 1994.

Nichols, Jerry. Officer with the Aurora (Colo.) Police Department K-9 Unit. Telephone interview with author, June 27, 1994.

(The following newspaper articles were taken from the files of the Aurora Police Department. In some cases, dates of publication were not available.)

Carnahan, Ann. "Strangers Join Friends, Family in Bittersweet Farewell to Alie," *Rocky Mountain News*, Denver, n.d.

Ensslin, John C. "Sadly, Dog's Perfect Record Still Stands," *Rocky Mountain News*, Denver, n.d.

Lopez, Greg. "Mom and Friends of Girl Wait, Watch and Worry," *Rocky Mountain News*, Denver, May 20, 1993.

Newcomer, Kris. "Cool, Rainy Weather Helps Bloodhounds Do Their Job," *Rocky Mountain News*, Denver, n.d.

O'Driscoll, Patrick, and Ann Schrader and Stacey Baca. "Massive Search for 'Alie' Berrelez Ends in Canyon of Rural Jeffco," *The Denver Post*, n.d.

Seipel, Tracy. "Yogi the Bloodhound 6 for 10 in Slaying Cases," *The Denver Post*, May 25, 1993.

"Yogi the Bloodhound is Colorado's Miracle Dog," *The Denver Post*, May 26, 1993.

INDEX

Ackerman, Jasper D., 58
Air Force Academy (Colorado Springs), 94
Alamosa, Colo., 78, 79, 81, 82, 85, 86, 87
Alamosa Chamber of Commerce, 85
Alamosa *Valley Courier*, 81
Alderdice, Suzannah, 3
Alie (bloodhound), 109
Alma, Colo., 28, 29, 30, 32, 34
Altshuler, Dr. John Henry, 82, 83
American Airlines, 69
An Alien Harvest, 82
Animal Reveille, 56
Anthony, James W., 16-18
Asher, James, 15
Aspen, Colo., 86
Aurora (Colo.) Police Dept., 104

Badger Creek, 13
Bancroft, Caroline, 31
Barney (bison), 95
Battle of Summit Springs, 2-6, 7
Beloit, Wis., 30
Berrelez, Alie, 103-106, 109
Billy (horse), 7
Bison, 91-97
Black Mountain, 14, 16, 17
Boise, Idaho, 16
Bone, Hamilton T. (mule), 55
Bonheur, Rosa, 7
Boulder, Colo., 62, 63, 92
Boulder *Daily Camera*, 93, 94
Brigham (horse), 6, 7
Broomfield, Colo., 62, 63, 64
Brown Palace Hotel (Denver), 74
Bruhn, Leander "Ole," 62, 65
Brunner, Dr. Clyde, 63, 64
Buckskin Joe (horse), 7
Buckskin Joe mine, 29, 30
Buena Vista, Colo., 71, 73, 74
Buffalo Bill (see Cody, William F.)

Buffy (bison), 95
Bugs (horse), 71
Buntline, Ned, 7
Burros, 27-35, 37-41

Cameron Mountain, 15
Camp Carson Hunt Club, 58
Canon City, Colo., 14, 16, 18
Capelli, Johnnie, 39, 40
Carr, Eugene, 1, 2, 4, 6
Carson, Fort (or Camp), 53, 55, 56, 57, 58, 59
Casotti, Fred, 91
Castle Air Force Base (Calif.), 59
Cattle, 21-25
Centennial Race Track (Denver area), 69, 73
Chatfield Reservoir, 105
Charlie (horse), 7, 8
Cherry Hills (Colo.) Police Dept., 109
Cheyenne Indians, 1-6
Cheyenne, Wyo., 54, 55
The Citizen, 61
Civil War, 56
Cody, William F., 1-8
Collegiate Range, 67
Colorado College, 18
Colorado Dept. of Transportation, 64
Colorado Highway Patrol, 63, 109
Colorado River, 99
Colorado Society for the Investigation of Unexplained Phenomenon, 83
Colorado Springs, Colo., 18, 59, 94, 107
Colorado Springs *Sun*, 53
Cory, John, 11, 12
Cotsiomitis, John, 74
CU Century, 91

Danny (sentry dog), 50
Day One, 106
Deer Creek Canyon, 105, 106

Dempewolff, Richard, 56, 57
Denny, Ray, 44
Denver, Colo., 8, 28, 30, 62, 73, 81, 105
Denver-Boulder Turnpike, 61, 64
The Denver Post, 18, 28, 30, 39, 44, 57, 67, 69-75, 84, 87, 103, 106, 108
Denver Times, 17
Desert Research Institute (Nev.), 87
Dogs, vi, 37-41, 43-50, 61-65, 99-101, 103-109
Dogs at War, 43
Dogs for Defense, 48
Dogs for Defense, Inc., 46-48
Dogs for Democracy, 50
Dolly Varden mine, 30
Douglas, John, 15
Downey, Fairfax, 48
Duke (horse), 7
Dummit (bear dog), 17
Duncan, Lon, 21, 22, 24, 25
Dutchess (dog), 99, 100

Englewood, Colo., 103, 104, 105, 106
Erlanger, Mrs. Milton S., 46

Fairplay, Colo., 13, 14, 27-34, 37-41
Fairplay Flume, 12
Fala (dog), 48
Falcon Stadium (Colorado Springs), 94
Fenwick, Red, 84-86
Fifth Cavalry, 1-3
Folsom Field (Boulder), 91
Forts (see specific names)
Fourth Field Artillery Battalion, 57
Fourth Infantry Division Artillery, 59
Franklin, Benjamin, 45

Ginger (bear dog), 17
Glenwood Springs, Colo., 99, 101
Going, Clayton G., 43
The Golden Transcript, 33
Graham, Robert, 1
Great Sand Dunes National Monument, 82
Grizzlies, vii, 11-19, 21-25
Guffey, Colo., 15
Gunnison, Colo., 14, 68, 71

Hale, Camp, 54, 55, 69
Hand Hotel (Fairplay), 39
Harvard, Mount, 67
Hidden Valley Ranch (Boulder area), 96
High Twelve mine, 38
Home Sweet Home mine, 30
Horses, 1-8, 67-75, 77-88
Howe, Linda Moulton, 82
Hubbard, W.P., 21, 23, 25

IM Ranch, 13
Indians (see specific tribes)
International Stock Show (Chicago), 55

Jefferson County, Colo., 108
Jorgensen, Ben, 68, 71
Just So Stories, 99

K-9 Corps, 44, 46, 48-50
Kansas Pacific Railroad, 6
King, Agnes, 80
King, Harry, 77, 78
Kipling, Rudyard, 99

Lady (horse), 77-88
Lakewood, Colo., 70
Lancaster, Dr. Ellsworth, 18, 19
Leadville, Colo., 14, 30
Leary, Dr. Wallace, 87-88
Leavenworth, Fort, 7
Legislature, Colorado, 106
Lewis, Berle, 78
Lewis, Nellie (Mrs. Berle), 78-80, 85, 87
Life magazine, 58, 70
Lookout Mountain, 8
Lord Byron, 37
Lubbock, Texas, 91

McPherson, Fort, 1
McWilliams, George, 69
Monte Vista, Colo., 14
Mosquito Gulch, 38
Mosquito mine, 30
Mules, 53-59
Museum of Vertebrate Zoology (Berkeley, Calif.), 18

National Investigations Committee on Aerial Phenomenon, 83
National Police Hall of Fame, 106
Nichols, Jerry, 104-109
Notorious Grizzly Bears, 21, 23

Park County, Colo., 29
Pawnee Indians, 2, 7
Pigg, Wharton, 14, 16-18
Pikes Peak or Bust Rodeo, 55, 58
Pikes Peak Range Ride, 59
Powder Face (horse), 7
Powell, Wallace, 67-69
Price, George, 3
The Pueblo Chieftain, 27, 77, 78-80, 81, 84

Quaker Oats Co., 100

Radliff, Jake, 11-14
Ralphie II (bison), 96, 97
Ralphie III (bison), 96
Ralphie IV (bison), 96
Ray (bear dog), 17
The Reader's Digest, 69
Reno, Fort, 56
Republican River, 1
Riley, Fort, 56, 58
Ring (bear dog), 17
Roberts, Laurie, 99, 100
Roberts, Rob, 99, 100
Rocky Mountain News (Denver), 65, 87
Roosevelt, Franklin D., 48
Russellville Historical Society, 109

San Luis Valley, 77, 80, 82, 86
Sangre de Cristo Mountains, 78, 82
Sedgwick, Fort, 3
Seymour, Henry, 11, 12
Shepard, Mrs. Nettie, 74
Sherwood, Rupert, 27-35
Sicily, invasion of, 43, 44
Sill, Fort, 56
Sioux Indians, 2
Smith, Columbus, 53
South Platte River, 2
Spirit (bison), 95
Stirrup Ranch, 14, 16, 18
Storke, Harry P., 54

Stout, Joanna, 34
Streaker (bison), 95
South London mine, 38
Summit Springs, Colo., 2

Talbot, C.W., 11
Tall Bull (Cheyenne chief), 1-6
Taylor, Ralph C., 27
Trotter (mule), 54, 55
Tucker (horse), 7
Turner, Al, 71-73
Turner, Bill, 71-74
Two Burros of Fairplay, 31
Two Crows (Cheyenne Indian), 3

UFOs, 80-83, 86, 88
United Nations, 70
University of Colorado, 86, 91-97
University of Nevada, 87
Ute Indians, 6

Veterans of Foreign Wars, 44

Warren, Gordon, 68, 69
Washington, George, 56
Weichel, Mrs. G., 3
West Point military academy, 55
Western State Aviation Service (Gunnison), 68
Wharton, Edith, vi
Wicks, Byron, 107
World War I, 32, 45
World War II, 43-50, 57
Wright & Morgan Market (Canon City), 18

Yale, Mount, 67
Yoseloff, Thomas, 50
Young, Brigham, 6

DISCOVER MORE OF COLORADO

Colorado on My Mind
Spectacular full-color photography and memorable quotes.
120 pp., 10 x 13", 140 color photos.

Colorado: A Postcard Book
Photography by Eric Wunrow
A beautiful way to keep in touch with family and friends. 22 color postcards, 7 x 5".

C is for Colorado
By Gayle C. Shirley
Illustrated by Constance R. Bergum
A delightful introduction to Colorado and the alphabet.
40 pp., 8 1/2 x 11" color illustrations.

It Happened in Colorado
By James C. Crutchfield
Thirty-four stories about events that shaped Colorado's history.
144 pp., 6 x 9", b&w illustrations.

Colorado Wildflowers
By Charlotte Jones
Illustrations by DD Dowden
Easy-to-understand identification suitable for young and old wildflower fans. 32 pp., 7 x 10", water-color illustrations.

FALCON GUIDES

Colorado Scenic Drives
By Stewart M. Green
262 pp., 6 x 9", b&w photos, maps, 8 pp. color section.

The Hiker's Guide to Colorado
By Caryn and Peter Boddie
296 pp., b&w photos, maps.

The Mountain Biker's Guide to Colorado
By Greg Bromka and Linda Gong
272 pp., 6 x 9", b&w photos, maps.

The Floater's Guide to Colorado
By Doug Wheat
296 pp., 6 x 9", b&w photos.

Colorado Wildlife Viewing Guide
By Mary Taylor Gray
128 pp., 6 x 9", color photos.

Visit your local bookstore for more information on these and other Falcon Press books or, call toll-free 1-800-582-2665.

FALCON